T0185583

SpringerBriefs in Computer Science

SpringerBriefs present concise summaries of cutting-edge research and practical applications across a wide spectrum of fields. Featuring compact volumes of 50 to 125 pages, the series covers a range of content from professional to academic.

Typical topics might include:

- A timely report of state-of-the art analytical techniques
- A bridge between new research results, as published in journal articles, and a contextual literature review
- A snapshot of a hot or emerging topic
- An in-depth case study or clinical example
- A presentation of core concepts that students must understand in order to make independent contributions

Briefs allow authors to present their ideas and readers to absorb them with minimal time investment. Briefs will be published as part of Springer's eBook collection, with millions of users worldwide. In addition, Briefs will be available for individual print and electronic purchase. Briefs are characterized by fast, global electronic dissemination, standard publishing contracts, easy-to-use manuscript preparation and formatting guidelines, and expedited production schedules. We aim for publication 8–12 weeks after acceptance. Both solicited and unsolicited manuscripts are considered for publication in this series.

This series is indexed in Scopus.

More information about this series at http://www.springer.com/series/10028

Felipe A. Louza • Simon Gog • Guilherme P. Telles

Construction of Fundamental Data Structures for Strings

 Springer

Felipe A. Louza
Faculty of Electrical Engineering
Federal University of Uberlândia
Uberlândia, Minas Gerais, Brazil

Simon Gog
eBay (United States)
San Jose, CA, USA

Guilherme P. Telles
Institute of Computing
University of Campinas
Campinas, São Paulo, Brazil

ISSN 2191-5768   ISSN 2191-5776   (electronic)
SpringerBriefs in Computer Science
ISBN 978-3-030-55107-0   ISBN 978-3-030-55108-7   (eBook)
https://doi.org/10.1007/978-3-030-55108-7

This Springer imprint is published by the registered company Springer Nature Switzerland AG
The registered company address is: Gewerbestrasse 11, 6330 Cham, Switzerland

Foreword

The field of algorithmics has recently seen the upsurge of *compressed data structures*, a family of data structures that take advantage of regularities in the data to use less space with only a negligible increase in the cost of the query operations. Bioinformatics is one of the fields where compressed data structures were first introduced: the successful sequencing of more and more genomes has caused a strong drive towards efficient algorithms for handling large genome datasets. In this scenario, compressed data structures were essential for storing such datasets in RAM achieving an order of magnitude improvement over disk-based data structures.

Today, compressed data structures are even more important: the Big Data revolution has shown that the power of an algorithm often depends on the amount of data it can handle. The ability of compressed data structures of dealing with more data essentially for free is a precious one. Indeed, we have witnessed to a widening of the scope of such data structures: originally introduced for sequences, they have been generalized to other discrete structures such as tree, graphs, permutations, etc.

This book deals with a fundamental issue for compressed data structures, namely their efficient construction. As compressed data structures should take advantage of any kind of regularity in the data, to build them we need a global view of the input. Unfortunately, compressed data structures are often used for huge datasets, so gaining a global view could be very expensive in terms of time and space. For this reason, there has been a large body of research devoted to the efficient construction of such data structures. When the data to be indexed is an integer sequence or a string, the construction of compressed data structures is usually done through an object called *suffix array*. The construction of the *suffix array* is a challenging problem that has seen considerable improvements since it was first posed 30 years ago. A milestone result was the introduction in 2013 of the *induced sorting* algorithm: an elegant recursive algorithm that runs in linear time and uses a negligible amount of working memory. The algorithm is also extremely fast in practice and has become the tool of choice for the construction of compressed data structures for strings and sequences.

This book shows how the techniques of *induced sorting* can be generalized to the construction of other important objects relevant to compressed data structures:

the *longest common prefix* (LCP) array, the *suffix array* for string collections, the *document array*, and the *Lyndon array*. All the proposed algorithms share the elegance and effectiveness of the original *induced sorting* algorithm, and they have been implemented and made available by the authors in libraries, which are extremely easy to use. In the book, the algorithms are described in a very clear style by providing detailed examples. For the quality of its content, I recommend the book to anyone interested in compressed data structures and string algorithms: researchers new in the field will find it a valuable introduction to the topic, while experienced researchers will get important insights that will likely yield to new results in this fascinating area.

University of Eastern Piedmont, Vercelli, Italy   Giovanni Manzini
IIT-CNR, Pisa, Italy
May 2020

Preface

This book is an extension of the Ph.D. dissertation of Dr. Felipe A. Louza submitted to the *Universidade Estadual de Campinas*, 2017, Brazil. This work was selected as one of the best in the 31st Theses and Dissertations Competition sponsored by the *Brazilian Computer Society* and also received the honorable mention from *CAPES Thesis Award*, 2018.

This book reviews recent theoretical and practical advances on the construction of fundamental data structures for strings, which play a central role in many algorithmic solutions for Bioinformatics, Information Retrieval and Data Compression, among others. Numerous examples are featured throughout this book, including graphic explanations of sophisticated algorithms, which provide a clearer understanding of the main algorithmic ideas. This book is intended for advanced undergraduate students, graduate students, researchers and practitioners from Computer Science and Bioinformatics with a strong interest in algorithmic topics.

Part of the material presented in Chaps. 4, 5 and 6 was first published in *Inf. Process. Lett.* (v. 118), *Theor. Comput. Sci.* (v. 678) and *Lect. Notes Comput. Sci.* (v. 11811), respectively, and republished here with the permission of the copyright holder.

We would like to thank the Brazilian people who supported the development of this book through the funding agencies *CAPES*, *CNPq* and *FAPESP*.

We also thank our coauthors Sabrina Mantaci, Giovanni Manzini and Marinella Sciortino who collaborated on the results presented in Chap. 6. Especially, we are grateful to Giovanni Manzini, for kindly writing the Foreword.

Finally, we would like to thank the *Universidade Federal de Uberlândia, Universidade Estadual de Campinas* and *eBay Inc.* for providing us a fruitful environment to work.

Uberlândia, Brazil   Felipe A. Louza

San Jose, CA, USA   Simon Gog

Campinas, Brazil   Guilherme P. Telles
May 2020

Contents

Part I
Introduction and Preliminaries

Chapter 1
Introduction

1.1 Motivation

Strings are prevalent in Computer Science and the design of algorithms and data
structures for their efficient processing are fundamental for solving theoretical and
applied problems in numerous applications of Information Retrieval, Bioinformatics, and Data Compression, among others.

In this book we review recent contributions to the construction of fundamental
data structures for strings. The construction of such structures is deeply connected
to solving the *suffix sorting problem*. This problem is central to the computation of
fundamental data structures for strings, such as the suffix array [8, 22], perhaps the
most versatile and interesting data structure for string processing. The suffix array
combined with related data structures may be used in many applications as building
blocks of strategies that process text datasets efficiently. In this chapter, we present
a brief introduction to suffix sorting and other related problems, and we highlight
data structures that were developed for their solution.

Finding all occurrences of a string (pattern) P, of length m, within another string
(text) T, of length n, is a problem that arises repeatedly in different contexts, often
as a primary operation in the solution of more elaborated tasks [12]. This problem
is known as the exact string matching, and it may be solved in $O(n + m)$ time by
classical, online algorithms [14]. However, in large-scale applications, where the
size of T is much larger than the size of P, and when T is to be matched many
times, such online solutions are impractical and alternatives that preprocess the text
to build an index are essential.

A text index is a data structure built over a text T, which allows efficiently solving
a large number of string processing problems. Such improvement generally comes
at the cost of additional space to store the complete index data structure. Recent
developments in modern text indexes aim at designing compact and succinct data

© The Author(s), under exclusive licence to Springer Nature Switzerland AG 2020
F. A. Louza et al., *Construction of Fundamental Data Structures for Strings*,
SpringerBriefs in Computer Science, https://doi.org/10.1007/978-3-030-55108-7_1

This is a text. A text has many words, words have many letters.

Fig. 1.1 Text in English

Fig. 1.2 Inverted index for
the text in Fig. 1.1

i	vocabulary	positions
1	a	9, 17
2	has	24
3	have	46
4	is	6
5	letters	56
6	many	28, 51
7	text	11, 19
8	this	1
9	words	33, 40

structures to provide efficient data manipulation and fast queries using as less space as possible [23].

The inverted index (or inverted file) [2] is the most popular text index. Given a text T and a collection of words W that occur in T, referred to as the vocabulary, the inverted index lists all positions where each distinct word of W appears in T, providing a simple and fast search engine for textual data [34]. Figure 1.2 shows the inverted index built for the text given in Fig. 1.1. The main limitation of the inverted index is that not always the input text can be divided into words to form the vocabulary. For example, DNA and protein sequences, and some Eastern natural languages like Chinese, Japanese, and Korean have no well-defined notion of word or phrase delimiters. There are also some agglutinating languages like Finnish or German, and Twitter *hashtags*, where dividing and finding out all distinct (sub) words can be a challenging task. Figures 1.3, 1.4, 1.5, and 1.6 show examples of such inputs.

A full-text index for text T references every possible substring of T, allowing queries for patterns of any length occurring at any position of the text. The suffix tree [33] is a classical full-text index that solves a myriad of string processing problems in optimal time, including the exact string matching in $O(m)$ time, independently of the length of T. The drawback of its usage, however, is the large space requirement which becomes impractical in real situations. Several space-efficient alternatives have been investigated to replace suffix trees by compact data structures [4, 11, 24, 31]. We refer the reader to the recent textbooks [21, 23, 27] for further examples and applications where full-text indexes are used for solving different string processing problems. At the very heart of the construction of modern full-text indexes is suffix sorting.

AAGAAAAGTATGACGAAGTATGACGAGGGGACGTAGAAAAAGTATGACGAGGACAGTATGA

Fig. 1.3 DNA sequence

我要一杯咖啡

Fig. 1.4 Text in Chinese that translates to "I would like a cup of coffee"

Donaudampfschifffahrtsgesellschaftskapitän

Fig. 1.5 Text in German that translates to "Danube steamship company captain"

#breakingtheworldrecordforlongesthashtagever

Fig. 1.6 Twitter hashtag

1.2 Suffix Sorting

Suffix sorting is a well-studied problem in string processing. Given a text T it aims at sorting the n suffixes of T in lexicographic order. Figure 1.7 shows the list of all suffixes for the text $T =$ banaananaanana$ in lexicographic order.

Suffix sorting differs from sorting a collection of arbitrary strings, in the sense that given two suffixes of T, one is always a substring of the other. Then by carefully arranging the computation of suffix order relations, suffix sorting can be done in linear time on the length n of T [13], while any general comparison-based algorithm, like merge-sort, would take $O(n^2 \log n)$ time to sort the suffixes [15].

The list of n integers denoting the starting positions of all sorted suffixes is known as the suffix array of T [8, 22]. All the occurrences of a pattern P in T can be found in $O(m \log n)$ time by a binary search on the suffix array. This time can be further reduced using auxiliary data structures.

Several suffix sorting algorithms have been proposed since the introduction of the suffix array (see the reviews [3, 29]). In 2009, Nong et al. [26] introduced a remarkable algorithm, called SAIS, that computes the suffix array in linear time using $0.5n + \sigma + O(1)$ words of additional memory, where a word has $\log n$ bits and σ is the string alphabet size. In 2013, Nong [25] presented an elegant variant of SAIS, called SACA-K, which runs in linear time using $\sigma + O(1)$ additional words. Nong's algorithm is optimal in time and space for alphabets of constant size, where $\sigma = O(1)$, as in DNA sequences ($\sigma = 4$), protein sequences, ($\sigma = 21$) and ASCII texts ($\sigma = 256$). More recently, Li et al. [16] and Goto [9] reduced the memory requirement of Nong's algorithm to $O(1)$ words, which is optimal for integer alphabets. Therefore, we may consider that the problem of computing the suffix array is essentially solved in the literature [13], even though the development of algorithms that are faster in practice is still an ongoing research (e.g. [1, 28, 30, 32]).

Recent advances in suffix sorting include the development of *augmented suffix sorting algorithms* that compute related data structures during the suffix array

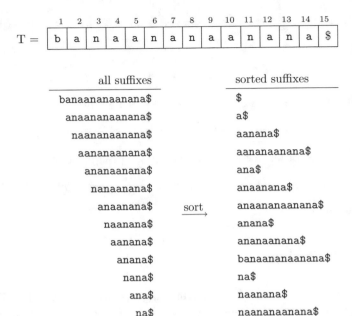

Fig. 1.7 Suffix sorting for $T = $ banaananaanana\$

construction, such as the longest common prefix (LCP) array and the document array (e.g. [5, 6, 9, 10, 17–20]). The LCP array holds the length of the longest common prefix between two consecutive sorted suffixes, while the document array stores which document each suffix in the lexicographic order belongs to. These data structures are building blocks of many modern compact full-text indexes [23].

Another important data structure for strings is the Lyndon array [7]. It provides information regarding the maximal periodicities occurring in a string. Algorithms that compute Lyndon arrays use the suffix array as an intermediate data structure. An interesting question is to devise augmented suffix sorting algorithms to compute both arrays simultaneously.

In this book, we review recent contributions in these topics, we present theoretical improvements and practical advances on augmented suffix sorting for building the suffix array together with related data structures.

1.3   Overview of the Book

This book is organized as follows:

Chap. 2:   Introduces background and notation used throughout this book.

Chap. 3: Reviews the suffix sorting problem and presents algorithms SAIS and SACA-K, which are the basis of the algorithms described in Chaps. 4, 5, and 6.

Chap. 4: Presents two algorithms that compute the LCP array as a by-product of algorithms SAIS and SACA-K. Experimental evaluation shows the overhead added by computing the LCP array.

Chap. 5: Presents two algorithms that compute the suffix array together with the document array for string collections. These algorithms build on SAIS and SACA-K, maintaining their bounds. Experiments demonstrate the outstanding practical performance of these algorithms.

Chap. 6: Presents an algorithm that computes the Lyndon array during the algorithm SACA-K in optimal time and space for strings from constant alphabets.

Chap. 7: Presents concluding remarks and outlines trends in suffix sorting.

References

1. J. Bahne, N. Bertram, M. Böcker, J. Bode, J. Fischer, H. Foot, F. Grieskamp, F. Kurpicz, M. Löbel, O. Magiera, R. Pink, D. Piper, C. Poeplau, Sacabench: benchmarking suffix array construction, in *Proc. International Symposium on String Processing and Information Retrieval (SPIRE)*, pp. 407–416 (2019)
2. A.F. Cardenas, Analysis and performance of inverted data base structures. Commun. ACM **18**(5), 253–263 (1975)
3. J. Dhaliwal, S.J. Puglisi, A. Turpin, Trends in suffix sorting: a survey of low memory algorithms, in *Proc. Australasian Computer Science Conference (ACSC)*, pp. 91–98 (2012)
4. P. Ferragina, G. Manzini, Indexing compressed text. J. ACM **52**(4), 552–581 (2005)
5. J. Fischer, Inducing the LCP-array, in *Proc. Workshop on Algorithms and Data Structures (WADS)*, pp. 374–385 (2011)
6. J. Fischer, F. Kurpicz, Dismantling divsufsort, in *Proc. Prague Stringology Conference (PSC)*, pp. 62–76 (2017)
7. F. Franek, A.S.M.S. Islam, M.S. Rahman, W.F. Smyth, Algorithms to compute the Lyndon array, in *Proc. Prague Stringology Conference (PSC)*, pp. 172–184 (2016)
8. G.H. Gonnet, R.A. Baeza-Yates, T. Snider, New indices for text: PAT trees and PAT arrays, in *Information Retrieval*, pp. 66–82 (Prentice-Hall, 1992)
9. K. Goto, Optimal time and space construction of suffix arrays and LCP arrays for integer alphabets, in *Proc. Prague Stringology Conference (PSC)*, pp. 111–125 (2019)
10. K. Goto, H. Bannai, Space efficient linear time Lempel-Ziv factorization for small alphabets, in *Proc. IEEE Data Compression Conference (DCC)*, pp. 163–172 (2014)
11. R. Grossi, J.S. Vitter, Compressed suffix arrays and suffix trees with applications to text indexing and string matching. SIAM J. Comput. **35**(2), 378–407 (2005)
12. D. Gusfield, *Algorithms on Strings, Trees and Sequences: Computer Science and Computational Biology* (Cambridge University Press, 1997)
13. J. Kärkkäinen, Suffix array construction, in *Encyclopedia of Algorithms*, pp. 2141–2144 (Springer, 2016)
14. D.E. Knuth, J.H. Morris, Jr., V.R. Pratt, Fast pattern matching in strings. SIAM J. Comput. **6**(2), 323–350 (1977)
15. N.J. Larsson, Notes on suffix sorting. Technical report, LU-CS-TR, Lund University, Sweden, 1998

16. Z. Li, J. Li, H. Huo, Optimal in-place suffix sorting, in *Proc. International Symposium on String Processing and Information Retrieval (SPIRE)*, pp. 268–284 (2018)
17. F.A. Louza, T. Gagie, G.P. Telles, Burrows-Wheeler transform and LCP array construction in constant space. J. Discrete Algorithms **42**, 14–22 (2017)
18. F.A. Louza, S. Gog, G.P. Telles, Inducing enhanced suffix arrays for string collections. Theor. Comput. Sci. **678**, 22–39 (2017)
19. F.A. Louza, S. Gog, G.P. Telles, Optimal suffix sorting and LCP array construction for constant alphabets. Inf. Process. Lett. **118**, 30–34 (2017)
20. F.A. Louza, S. Mantaci, G. Manzini, M. Sciortino, G.P. Telles, Inducing the Lyndon array, in *Proc. International Symposium on String Processing and Information Retrieval (SPIRE)*, pp. 138–151 (2019)
21. V. Mäkinen, D. Belazzougui, F. Cunial, A.I. Tomescu, *Genome-Scale Algorithm Design* (Cambridge University Press, 2015)
22. U. Manber, G. Myers, Suffix arrays: a new method for on-line string searches, in *Proc. ACM-SIAM Symposium on Discrete Algorithms (SODA)*, pp. 319–327 (1990)
23. G. Navarro, *Compact Data Structures: A Practical Approach* (Cambridge University Press, 2016)
24. G. Navarro, V. Mäkinen, Compressed full-text indexes. ACM Comput. Surv. **39**(1), 1–61 (2007)
25. G. Nong, Practical linear-time O(1)-workspace suffix sorting for constant alphabets. ACM Trans. Inf. Syst. **31**(3), 1–15 (2013)
26. G. Nong, S. Zhang, W.H. Chan, Linear suffix array construction by almost pure induced-sorting, in *Proc. IEEE Data Compression Conference (DCC)*, pp. 193–202 (2009)
27. E. Ohlebusch, *Bioinformatics Algorithms: Sequence Analysis, Genome Rearrangements and Phylogenetic Reconstruction* (Oldenbusch Verlag, 2013)
28. Z. Peng, Y. Wang, X. Xue, J. Wei, An efficient algorithm for suffix sorting. Int. J. Pattern Recognit. Artif. Intell. **30**(6), 1659018 (2016)
29. S.J. Puglisi, W.F. Smyth, A.H. Turpin, A taxonomy of suffix array construction algorithms. ACM Comput. Surv. **39**(2), 1–31 (2007)
30. S. Rajasekaran, M. Nicolae, An elegant algorithm for the construction of suffix arrays. J. Discrete Algorithms **27**, 21–28 (2014)
31. K. Sadakane, Compressed suffix trees with full functionality. Theory Comput. Syst. **41**(4), 589–607 (2007)
32. N. Timoshevskaya, W.C. Feng, SAIS-OPT: on the characterization and optimization of the SA-IS algorithm for suffix array construction, in *Proc. International Conference on Computational Advances in Bio and Medical Sciences (ICCABS)*, pp. 1–6 (2014)
33. P. Weiner, Linear pattern matching algorithms, in *Proc. Annual Symposium on Switching and Automata Theory (SWAT)*, pp. 1–11 (1973)
34. I.H. Witten, A. Moffat, T.C. Bell, *Managing Gigabytes: Compressing and Indexing Documents and Images*, 2nd edn. (Morgan Kaufmann, 1999)

Chapter 2
Background

2.1 Definitions and Notation

Strings are present in many applications of Computer Science and details on their definitions and notation may vary depending on the context of the application. In this section we present basic notation used throughout this book.

2.1.1 Alphabets

Definition 2.1 An *alphabet* Σ is a totally ordered set of elements called symbols (or characters or letters). We denote the size of Σ by $|\Sigma| = \sigma$.

The alphabet size is important in the analysis of algorithms in this book, since most of them depend on the alphabet size. We assume that for any $\alpha_i, \alpha_j \in \Sigma$ it takes constant time to decide whether $\alpha_i < \alpha_j$ or $\alpha_i = \alpha_j$ or $\alpha_i > \alpha_j$.

Example The DNA alphabet $\Sigma = \{A, C, G, T\}$, with $\sigma = 4$ symbols, has the standard order $A < C < G < T$ among its elements.

2.1.2 Strings

Definition 2.2 A *string* (or text or sequence) T is a finite sequence of n symbols $T[1]T[2]\ldots T[n]$ from alphabet Σ, where $T[i]$ denotes the i-th symbol of T, with $1 \leq 1 \leq n$. We denote the length of T by $|T| = n$.

Definition 2.3 Given an alphabet Σ of size σ, we say that Σ is *constant* if $\sigma = O(1)$, otherwise, if $\sigma = n^{O(1)}$, we say that Σ is *integer*.

© The Author(s), under exclusive licence to Springer Nature Switzerland AG 2020
F. A. Louza et al., *Construction of Fundamental Data Structures for Strings*,
SpringerBriefs in Computer Science, https://doi.org/10.1007/978-3-030-55108-7_2

We assume that T always ends with a special symbol $T[n] = \$$, called *sentinel*, which is not present elsewhere in T and is smaller than any other symbol in Σ. The following consequences of sentinels' existence are technically convenient in simplifying definitions and algorithms: since no suffix of T can be a prefix of another suffix of T and the suffixes of T are pairwise distinct.

The *concatenation* of two strings is the string resulting of appending the second string at the end of the first. Most of the times we indicate concatenation as juxtaposition.

Definition 2.4 A *substring* of T is defined as $T[i, j] = T[i] \ldots T[j]$, with $1 \leq i < j \leq n$. In particular, $T[1, i]$ is a *prefix* of T and $T[i, n]$ is a *suffix* of T, with $1 \leq i \leq n$. For a clearer notation, we will denote suffix $T[i, n]$ by T_i.

The words "sequence" and "string" are synonymous in the literature, but "subsequence" and "substring" are not. The former may have non-consecutive symbols of T, whereas in the latter the symbols must be consecutive.

Example Given $T = $ banana\$, we have nana as both a substring and a subsequence of T, whereas aaa is a subsequence, but not a substring of T.

Definition 2.5 The *i-th rotation* of a string $T[1, n]$ is the string $T[i + 1] \ldots T[n]T[1] \ldots T[i]$. A rotation is also referred to as *circular rotation* or *conjugate*.

Example Given $T = $ banana\$, its rotations are anana\$b, nana\$ba, ana\$ban, na\$bana, a\$banan, and \$banana.

2.1.3   Model of Computation

Throughout this book we assume the standard RAM model of computation. We assume that the length of the text to be processed may be stored into a single word. We will express algorithms' space requirements in terms of either words or bits.

We assume that the alphabet Σ is constant most of the time, with size $\sigma < 256$, as in DNA sequences ($\sigma = 4$), protein sequences ($\sigma = 21$), and ASCII texts ($\sigma = 128$). Then, each symbol $T[i]$ is stored in one byte and any string $T[1, n]$ is stored within n bytes.

We assume that an integer value in the range $[1, n]$ can be stored in one model word (four bytes when $n < 2^{32}$, and eight bytes, otherwise). Any array of integers $A[1, n]$ with values in the range $[1, n]$ is stored within n words.

Definition 2.6 The *workspace* (or working space) of an algorithm is the extra space used in addition to the memory needed by the input text T and the output data structure.

Example Given an algorithm that needs an auxiliary array of integers $A[1, n]$ plus a couple of variables on top of the input and the output, we may say that its workspace is $n + O(1)$ words.

2.2 Data Structures for Strings

The suffix array, the longest common prefix array, and the document array are fundamental data structures that are at the very heart of many modern compact full-text indexes. Despite their simplicity, these data structures play a central role also in data compression and combinatorics on words [36, 46, 49].

It is noteworthy stressing that the *suffix tree* [59] is a classical full-text index that allows solving a myriad of string processing problems in optimal time. However, due to its large memory requirements, suffix trees are not used in practice.

We adopt the typographic convention of using sans-serif faces when referring to data structures. For instance, the suffix array will be abbreviated as SA and will be denoted by SA in mathematical expressions.

2.2.1 Suffix Array

The suffix array (SA) was introduced by Manber and Myers [37, 38] as a space-efficient alternative to the classical suffix tree [59]. Gonnet and Baeza-Yates [20] independently proposed an equivalent data structure, called *Patricia* (PAT) array, for building an index for the Oxford English Dictionary project.

Definition 2.7 The *suffix array* of a string $T[1, n]$, denoted by SA, is an array of distinct integers in the range $[1, n]$ that provides the positions of the suffixes of T in lexicographic order, that is,

$$T_{\mathsf{SA}[1]} < T_{\mathsf{SA}[2]} < \ldots < T_{\mathsf{SA}[n]}.$$

Example Figure 2.1 shows the suffix array for T — banaananaanana\$. The figure also shows other data structures to be introduced soon.

Finding all occurrences of a pattern $P[1, m]$ in T can be done in $O(m \log n)$ time by performing a binary search on $\mathsf{SA}[1, n]$. This time can be reduced to $O(m + \log n)$ by using additional data structures.

There are several suffix sorting algorithms to compute the SA, see the reviews [11, 52]. The suffix array can be constructed in linear time using $\sigma + O(1)$ words of workspace [48], which is optimal for constant alphabets.

A suffix array may be partitioned according to the first symbol of each suffix. Blocks in this partition are important in suffix array construction algorithms.

Definition 2.8 A c-bucket is a block of a partition of $\mathsf{SA}[1, n]$ where all suffixes start with the same symbol $c, c \in \Sigma$.

Example Figure 2.1 shows all c-buckets separated by dashed lines for the suffix array computed for $T = $ banaananaanana\$.

	1	2	3	4	5	6	7	8	9	10	11	12	13	14	15
$T =$	b	a	n	a	a	n	a	n	a	a	n	a	n	a	$

	SA	LCP	BWT	suffixes
1	15	0	a	$
2	14	0	n	a$
3	9	1	n	aanana$
4	4	6	n	aananaanana$
5	12	1	n	ana$
6	7	3	n	anaanana$
7	2	8	b	anaananaanana$
8	10	3	a	anana$
9	5	5	a	ananaanana$
10	1	0	$	banaananaanana$
11	13	0	a	na$
12	8	2	a	naanana$
13	3	7	a	naananaanana$
14	11	2	a	nana$
15	6	4	a	nanaanana$

Fig. 2.1 Suffix array, LCP array, and BWT for $T =$ banaananaanana$. The c-buckets of SA are separated by dashed lines

2.2.1.1　Inverse Suffix Array and Φ-Array

Some relations among suffixes are defined through the inverse suffix array and through the Φ-array. The inverse suffix array (ISA) provides the position of SA that indexes T_i.

Definition 2.9 The *inverse suffix array*, denoted by ISA, is an array of integers in the range $[1, n]$, such that

$$\text{ISA}[i] = j \text{ if and only if } \text{SA}[j] = i.$$

The Φ-array provides the index of the suffix that precedes T_i in SA.

Definition 2.10 The Φ-*array* is an array of integers in the range $[1, n]$, such that

$$\Phi[i] = \begin{cases} \text{SA}[\text{ISA}[i] - 1] & \text{if ISA}[i] \neq 1 \\ 0 & \text{otherwise.} \end{cases}$$

The inverse suffix array and the Φ-array can be obtained from the suffix array in linear time using $O(1)$ workspace [52].

2.2.1.2   Burrows–Wheeler Transform

The *Burrows–Wheeler transform* (BWT) [7] is a well-studied text transformation that permutes the symbols of a string T into another string T^{BWT} that often allows for better compression [40].

The BWT is defined by means of the sorted rotations of a text T, and can also be defined in terms of the suffix array of T as follows.

Definition 2.11 The BWT of a string $T[1, n]$, denoted by $T^{\mathsf{BWT}}[1, n]$, is a string with a permutation of the symbols of T such that

$$T^{\mathsf{BWT}}[i] = \begin{cases} T[\mathsf{SA}[i] - 1] & \text{if } \mathsf{SA}[i] \neq 1 \\ \$ & \text{otherwise.} \end{cases} \tag{2.1}$$

Therefore, the BWT can be easily obtained by first constructing the suffix array. The main disadvantage of this approach is that it requires at least n words to construct and store $\mathsf{SA}[1, n]$. Nonetheless, this alternative is still the fastest. The BWT can be also computed directly from T in linear time using $O(n \log \sigma)$ bits of workspace [18, 44]. The BWT can be computed directly in-place, that is, within the same space of the input text, but in quadratic time [9].

The BWT was proposed in the 1990s in the context of data compression.[1] Almost 10 years later, Ferragina and Manzini [14] showed that the BWT can be used to construct compact full-text indexes. This result opened new research opportunities, and nowadays the BWT is one of the main components of many modern compact indexes [46].

Example Figure 2.1 shows the BWT for $T = \mathsf{banaananaanana\$}$. Notice the clustering effect on the symbols in $T^{\mathsf{BWT}} = \mathsf{annnnnbaa\$aaaaa}$, where we have runs of n's and of a's.

2.2.2   *LCP Array*

The *longest common prefix* (LCP) array was introduced by Manber and Myers [37] by the name of Hgt-array to speed up the string matching over SA to $O(m + \log n)$ time at the cost of storing additional information.

---

[1]The BWT is the base of the popular data compression tool BZIP2 [54], see the textbook [2] for historical notes.

Definition 2.12 Let $\mathsf{lcp}(T^1, T^2)$ be the length of the longest common prefix (lcp) of two strings T^1 and T^2.

Definition 2.13 The *longest common prefix array*, denoted by LCP, is an array of integers in the range $[0, n-1]$ that stores the lcp of consecutive suffixes in SA, that is

$$\mathsf{LCP}[i] = \mathsf{lcp}(T_{\mathsf{SA}[i]}, T_{\mathsf{SA}[i-1]}), \text{ for } 1 < i \leq n, \text{ and } \mathsf{LCP}[1] = 0.$$

We define the permuted LCP array, which provides the lcp between T_i and T_{i-1}, as follows [25].

Definition 2.14 The *permuted LCP array*, denoted by PLCP, is an array of integers, such that

$$\mathsf{PLCP}[i] = \mathsf{LCP}[\mathsf{ISA}[i]].$$

Equivalently, PLCP can be defined in terms of the Φ-array.

$$\mathsf{PLCP}[i] = \mathsf{lcp}(T_i, T_{\Phi[i]}).$$

Arrays $\mathsf{LCP}[1, n]$ and $\mathsf{PLCP}[1, n]$ can be stored within n words each, since their values are bounded by n. In practice, for some specific domains like genome sequences and natural language texts, the expected value for each LCP value is $O(\log n)$ [46]. Thus, there exist alternatives to represent the LCP information using less than n words, most of them storing the PLCP array instead (e.g. [15, 25, 53]), which allows achieving a better compression rate. However, in virtually all applications the LCP values are required to be in suffix array order, and the PLCP is converted to the LCP array [19]. Other alternatives for encoding the LCP array preserve its elements' order [1, 6, 29].

The LCP array can be computed in linear time given the text and its suffix array as input using $O(n)$ words of workspace [25, 26, 42], or given only the BWT as input using $o(n)$ words [51], or alternatively, during the suffix array construction using $\sigma + O(1)$ words [31], which is optimal for constant alphabets.

The LCP values per se can provide useful information on the repetitiveness of a text [41], extending their role beyond indexing.

2.2.2.1 Longest Common Prefix

Given a string T and its LCP array, the lcp between any two suffixes in SA order is given by a *range minimum query* (rmq) on LCP.

Definition 2.15 We define $\mathsf{rmq}(i, j) = \min_{i < k \leq j}\{\mathsf{LCP}[k]\}$.

It is easy to see that $\mathsf{lcp}(T_{\mathsf{SA}[i]}, T_{\mathsf{SA}[j]}) = \mathsf{rmq}(i, j)$.

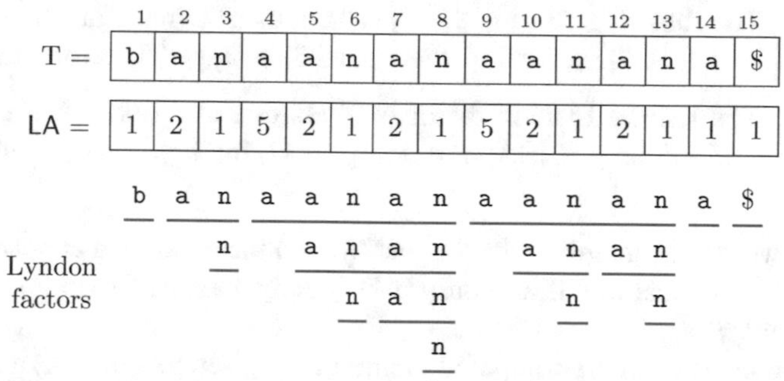

	1	2	3	4	5	6	7	8	9	10	11	12	13	14	15
T =	b	a	n	a	a	n	a	n	a	a	n	a	n	a	$
LA =	1	2	1	5	2	1	2	1	5	2	1	2	1	1	1

b a n a a n a n a a n a n a $

  n   a n a n   a n a n

    n a n   n   n

      n

Lyndon factors

Fig. 2.2 Lyndon array and Lyndon factors of $T =$ banaananaanana\$. The longest Lyndon factors starting at each position of T are underlined and shown at the bottom

Example Figure 2.1 illustrates the LCP array for $T =$ banaananaanana\$. Note that $\mathsf{lcp}(T_{\mathsf{SA}[7]}, T_{\mathsf{SA}[9]}) = \mathsf{rmq}(7, 9) = 3$ is equal to the lcp between suffixes T_2 and T_5.

2.2.3 Lyndon Array

A *Lyndon word* is a string that is lexicographically smaller than all of its rotations [35]. A *Lyndon factor* of a string T is a substring of T that is a Lyndon word.

Example For instance, the string $T =$ banaananaanana\$ is not a Lyndon word, because its 3-rd rotation aananaanana\$ban is smaller than $T[1, n]$. Also, the substrings b, an, n, and aanan are Lyndon factors that start at the four first positions of T.

The Lyndon array (LA) [16], also referred to as Lyndon table, is a powerful data structure that generalizes the idea of Lyndon factorization [12] as follows.

Definition 2.16 The Lyndon array of a string T, denoted by LA, is an array of integers in the range $[1, n]$ that, at each position $i = 1, \ldots, n$, stores the length of the longest Lyndon factor starting at $T[i]$:

$$\mathsf{LA}[i] = \max\{\ell \mid T[i, i + \ell - 1] \text{ is a Lyndon word}\}.$$

In 2017, Bannai et al. [5] used Lyndon arrays to prove that the number of maximal periodicities in a string of length n is smaller than n, which had been conjectured 20 years earlier by Kolpakov and Kucherov [27].

Example Figure 2.2 shows the Lyndon array and all Lyndon factors of $T =$ banaananaanana\$.

We can also define the Lyndon array in terms of SA and ISA [23], as follows.

Remark 2.1 The substring $T[i, i + \ell - 1]$ is the longest Lyndon factor of T starting at i if and only if $T_i < T_{i+k}$, for $1 \leq k < \ell$, and $T_i > T_{i+\ell}$. Therefore, $\mathsf{LA}[i] = \ell$.

Remark 2.2 The longest Lyndon factor of T starting at i is $T[i, i + \ell - 1]$, that is, $\mathsf{LA}[i] = \ell$, if and only if $\mathsf{ISA}[i] < \mathsf{ISA}[i + k]$, for $1 \leq k < \ell$, and $\mathsf{ISA}[i] > \mathsf{ISA}[i + \ell]$.

In other words, the length of the longest Lyndon factor starting at position i in T, namely $\mathsf{LA}[i]$, is equal to ℓ if and only if $T_{i+\ell}$ is the next suffix (in text order) that is smaller than T_i.

The Lyndon array can be computed in linear time given SA (or ISA) as input [16]. Alternatively, the LA can be computed from the Cartesian tree [58] built for the ISA [10]. Recently, Franek et al. [17] observed that the LA can be computed in linear time during the suffix array construction algorithm by Baier [4], and Louza et al. [32] showed how to modify Nong's algorithm [48] to compute the LA in linear time using $\sigma + O(1)$ words. The LA can also be computed in linear time during the Burrows–Wheeler inversion [33] using $3n + O(1)$ words on top of the space needed for T^{BWT} and $\mathsf{LA}[1, n]$.

2.2.4 Document Array

Let $\mathcal{T} = T^1, T^2, \ldots, T^d$ be a collection of d strings of lengths $n_1, n_2, \ldots, n_d$.

Definition 2.17 The suffix array of $\mathcal{T}$ is the suffix array built for the concatenation of all strings $T^{cat}[1, N] = T^1 T^2 \ldots T^d \#$ with total length $N = \sum_{i=1}^{d}(n_1) + 1$, where $\# < \$$ is a new sentinel symbol.

The suffix array for a collection $\mathcal{T}$ is sometimes referred to as *generalized suffix array* in the literature [55]. We use this name for an array of pairs of integers, to be introduced in the next section.

The suffix array for a collection $\mathcal{T}$ can be computed in $O(N)$ time using $\sigma + O(1)$ words of workspace [30] in such a way that ties between equal suffixes from different strings T^i and T^j are broken by their ranks i and j.

The LCP array and the BWT may also be constructed for string collections [8, 39]. The lcp values may not exceed separators ($-symbols) in $T^{cat}[1, N]$, while the BWT may be obtained through Eq. 2.1.

Example Figure 2.3 shows the suffix array, the LCP array, and the BWT for the string collection $\mathcal{T} = \{\text{banana}\$, \text{anaba}\$, \text{anan}\$\}$ concatenated into $T^{cat} = \text{banana}\$\text{anaba}\$\text{anan}\$\#$. The figure also shows other data structures to be introduced next.

The suffix array is commonly accompanied by the document array (DA) [45] when indexing string collections, defined as follows.

	1	2	3	4	5	6	7	8	9	10	11	12	13	14	15	16	17	18	19
$T^{cat} =$	b	a	n	a	n	a	\$	a	n	a	b	a	\$	a	n	a	n	\$	#

	SA	LCP	DA	GSA	BWT	suffixes
1	19	0	4	(4, 1)	\$	#
2	7	0	1	(1, 7)	a	\$
3	13	0	2	(2, 6)	a	\$
4	18	0	3	(3, 5)	n	\$
5	6	0	1	(1, 6)	n	a\$
6	12	1	2	(2, 5)	b	a\$
7	10	1	2	(2, 3)	n	aba\$
8	16	1	3	(3, 3)	n	an\$
9	4	2	1	(1, 4)	n	ana\$
10	8	3	2	(2, 1)	\$	anaba\$
11	14	3	3	(3, 1)	\$	anan\$
12	2	4	1	(1, 2)	b	anana\$
13	11	0	2	(2, 4)	a	ba\$
14	1	2	1	(1, 1)	#	banana\$
15	17	0	3	(3, 4)	0	n\$
16	5	1	1	(1, 5)	a	na\$
17	9	2	2	(2, 2)	a	naba\$
18	15	2	3	(3, 2)	a	nan\$
19	3	3	1	(1, 3)	a	nana\$

Fig. 2.3 Suffix array, LCP array, document array, generalized suffix array, and BWT for $T^{cat} =$ banana\$anaba\$anan\$#. The c-buckets of SA are separated by dashed lines

Definition 2.18 The document array, denoted by DA, is an array of integers that stores which document each suffix in SA belongs to, that is

$$\mathsf{DA}[i] = j \text{ if suffix } T^{cat}[\mathsf{SA}[i], N] \text{ came from string } T^j.$$

We define $\mathsf{DA}[1] = d + 1$ for the last suffix $T_N^{cat} = \text{\#}$.

The array $\mathsf{DA}[1, N]$ needs $N \lg(d+1)$ bits of space, which fits in N words. It may also be represented in a compact form by using a bitvector [49, Section 7.7], or by using *wavelet trees* [21], within the same space but with more functionalities [57]. $\mathsf{DA}[1, N]$ can be efficiently compressed using grammars when the string collection is repetitive [47]. In many situations (e.g. [3, 13, 22, 34, 50, 56]), the DA is scanned sequentially and having it explicitly stored in the array DA$[1, N]$ is important for good performance [28].

The document array can be computed given $T^{cat}[1, N]$ and its SA in the space of DA$[1, N]$ in linear time. First, a bitvector B$[1, N]$ is prepared for $O(1)$ time rank queries [43], such that,

$$B[i] = 1 \text{ if and only if } T^{cat}[i] = \$ \text{ and } B[i] = 0, \text{ otherwise.}$$

Then, for $i = 1, 2, \ldots, N$, DA$[i]$ may be obtained through [49, Alg. 7.29]:

$$DA[i] = rank_1(B, SA[i]) + 1,$$

where $rank_1(B, SA[i])$ returns the number of 1's in B$[1, SA[i]]$.

This algorithm runs in $O(N)$ time and needs $N + o(N)$ bits of workspace for the bitvector with rank support (see [49, Alg.7.29]).

Alternatively, DA can be computed during the suffix array construction in $O(N)$ time using $\sigma + O(1)$ words of workspace [30], which is optimal for strings from constant alphabets.

2.2.5   Generalized Suffix Array

The *generalized suffix array* (GSA) is as an array of N pairs of integers (a, b), denoted by GSA, such that each entry (a, b) represents suffix $T^a[b, n_a]$, with $1 \leq a \leq d$ and $1 \leq b \leq n_a$ [55]. In words, GSA gives the order of the suffixes of all strings in collection $\mathcal{T}$.

The GSA of two strings T^1, T^2 can be obtained in linear time by merging their individual suffix arrays [24], while the GSA for strings $T^1, T^2, \ldots, T^d$ can be obtained from arrays SA and DA as follows.

Given SA and DA, one can derive the entries $i = 1, 2, \ldots, N$ of GSA in linear time [30] as

$$GSA[i] = \begin{cases} (DA[i], SA[i] - SA[DA[i]]) & \text{if } DA[i] > 1 \\ (DA[i], SA[i]) & \text{otherwise.} \end{cases}$$

Also, given GSA, one can obtain SA and DA entries easily, as

$$SA[i] = \begin{cases} GSA[i](a) & \text{if } GSA[i](b) = 1 \\ GSA[i](a) + GSA[i](b)[GSA[i](b) - 1] + 1 & \text{otherwise} \end{cases}$$

$$DA[i] = GSA[i](b).$$

Indeed, the array GSA[1, N] is equivalent to the combined arrays SA and DA, such that algorithms for one representation can often be directly adapted to the other.

Example Figure 2.3 shows the suffix array (SA), the LCP array, the document array (DA), the generalized suffix array (GSA), and the BWT for the string collection $\mathcal{T} = \{\texttt{banana\$, anaba\$, anan\$}\}$.

References

1. M.I. Abouelhoda, S. Kurtz, E. Ohlebusch, Replacing suffix trees with enhanced suffix arrays. J. Discrete Algorithms **2**(1), 53–86 (2004)
2. D. Adjeroh, T. Bell, A. Mukherjee, *The Burrows-Wheeler Transform: Data Compression, Suffix Arrays and Pattern Matching* (Springer Publishing Company, Boston, MA, 2008)
3. M. Arnold, E. Ohlebusch, Linear time algorithms for generalizations of the longest common substring problem. Algorithmica **60**(4), 806–818 (2011)
4. U. Baier, Linear-time suffix sorting - a new approach for suffix array construction, in *Proc. Annual Symposium on Combinatorial Pattern Matching (CPM)*, pp. 23:1–23:12 (2016)
5. H. Bannai, I. Tomohiro, S. Inenaga, Y. Nakashima, M. Takeda, K. Tsuruta, The "runs" theorem. SIAM J. Comput. **46**(5), 1501–1514 (2017)
6. N.R. Brisaboa, S. Ladra, G. Navarro, DACs: bringing direct access to variable-length codes. Inf. Process. Lett. **49**(1), 392–404 (2013)
7. M. Burrows, D.J. Wheeler, A block-sorting lossless data compression algorithm. Technical report, Digital SRC Research Report, 1994
8. A.J. Cox, F. Garofalo, G. Rosone, M. Sciortino, Lightweight LCP construction for very large collections of strings. J. Discrete Algorithms **37**, 17–33 (2016)
9. M. Crochemore, R. Grossi, J. Kärkkäinen, G.M. Landau, Computing the Burrows-Wheeler transform in place and in small space. J. Discrete Algorithms **32**, 44–52 (2015)
10. M. Crochemore, L.M.S. Russo, Cartesian and Lyndon trees. Theor. Comput. Sci. (2018)
11. J. Dhaliwal, Faster semi-external suffix sorting. Inf. Process. Lett. **114**(4), 174–178 (2014)
12. J.P. Duval, Factorizing words over an ordered alphabet. J. Algorithms **4**(4), 363–381 (1983)
13. L. Egidi, F.A. Louza, G. Manzini, G.P. Telles, External memory BWT and LCP computation for sequence collections with applications. Algorithms Mol. Biol. **14**(1), 6:1–6:15 (2019)
14. P. Ferragina, G. Manzini, Opportunistic data structures with applications, in *Proc. Annual IEEE Symposium on Foundations of Computer Science (FOCS)*, pp. 390–398 (2000)
15. J. Fischer, Wee LCP. Inf. Process. Lett. **110**(8–9), 317–320 (2010)
16. F. Franek, A.S.M. Sohidull Islam, M.S. Rahman, W.F. Smyth, Algorithms to compute the Lyndon array, in *Proc. Prague Stringology Conference (PSC)*, pp. 172–184 (2016)
17. F. Franek, A. Paracha, W.F. Smyth, The linear equivalence of the suffix array and the partially sorted Lyndon array, in *Proc. Prague Stringology Conference (PSC)*, pp. 77–84 (2017)
18. J. Fuentes-Sepúlveda, G. Navarro, Y. Nekrich, Space-efficient computation of the Burrows-Wheeler transform, in *Proc. IEEE Data Compression Conference (DCC)*, pp. 132–141 (2019)
19. S. Gog, E. Ohlebusch, Compressed suffix trees: efficient computation and storage of LCP-values. J. Exp. Algorithmics (2013)
20. G.H. Gonnet, R.A. Baeza-Yates, T. Snider, New indices for text: PAT trees and PAT arrays, in *Information Retrieval*, pp. 66–82 (Prentice-Hall, 1992)
21. R. Grossi, A. Gupta, J.S. Vitter, High-order entropy-compressed text indexes, in *Proc. ACM-SIAM Symposium on Discrete Algorithms (SODA)*, pp. 841–850 (2003)
22. V. Guerrini, G. Rosone, Lightweight metagenomic classification via eBWT, in *Proc. International Conference on Algorithms for Computational Biology (AICoB)*, pp. 112–124 (2019)

23. C. Hohlweg, C. Reutenauer, Lyndon words, permutations and trees. Theor. Comput. Sci. **307**(1), 173–178 (2003)

24. J.-E. Jeon, H. Park, D.-K. Kim, Efficient construction of generalized suffix arrays by merging suffix arrays. J. KIISE Comput. Syst. Theory **32**(6), 268–278 (2005)

25. J. Kärkkäinen, G. Manzini, S.J. Puglisi, Permuted longest-common-prefix array, in *Proc. Annual Symposium on Combinatorial Pattern Matching (CPM)*, pp. 181–192 (2009)

26. T. Kasai, G. Lee, H. Arimura, S. Arikawa, K. Park, Linear-time longest-common-prefix computation in suffix arrays and its applications, in *Proc. Annual Symposium on Combinatorial Pattern Matching (CPM)*, pp. 181–192 (2001)

27. R.M. Kolpakov, G. Kucherov, Finding maximal repetitions in a word in linear time, in *Proc. Annual IEEE Symposium on Foundations of Computer Science (FOCS)*, pp. 596–604 (1999)

28. F.A. Louza, A simple algorithm for computing the document array. Inf. Process. Lett. **154** (2020)

29. F.A. Louza, T. Gagie, G.P. Telles, Burrows-Wheeler transform and LCP array construction in constant space. J. Discrete Algorithms **42**, 14–22 (2017)

30. F.A. Louza, S. Gog, G.P. Telles, Inducing enhanced suffix arrays for string collections. Theor. Comput. Sci. **678**, 22–39 (2017)

31. F.A. Louza, S. Gog, G.P. Telles, Optimal suffix sorting and LCP array construction for constant alphabets. Inf. Process. Lett. **118**, 30–34 (2017)

32. F.A. Louza, S. Mantaci, G. Manzini, M. Sciortino, G.P. Telles, Inducing the Lyndon array, in *Proc. International Symposium on String Processing and Information Retrieval (SPIRE)*, pp. 138–151 (2019)

33. F.A. Louza, W.F. Smyth, G. Manzini, G.P. Telles, Lyndon array construction during Burrows-Wheeler inversion. J. Discrete Algorithms **50**, 2–9 (2018)

34. F.A. Louza, G.P. Telles, S. Gog, L. Zhao, Algorithms to compute the Burrows-Wheeler similarity distribution. Theor. Comput. Sci. **782**, 145–156 (2019)

35. R.C. Lyndon, On Burnside's problem. Trans. Am. Math. Soc. **77**(2), 202–215 (1954)

36. V. Mäkinen, D. Belazzougui, F. Cunial, A.I. Tomescu, *Genome-Scale Algorithm Design* (Cambridge University Press, 2015)

37. U. Manber, G. Myers, Suffix arrays: a new method for on-line string searches, in *Proc. ACM-SIAM Symposium on Discrete Algorithms (SODA)*, pp. 319–327 (1990)

38. U. Manber, G. Myers, Suffix arrays: a new method for on-line string searches. SIAM J. Comput. **22**(5), 935–948 (1993)

39. S. Mantaci, A. Restivo, G. Rosone, M. Sciortino, An extension of the Burrows-Wheeler transform. Theor. Comput. Sci. **387**(3), 298–312 (2007)

40. G. Manzini, An analysis of the Burrows-Wheeler transform. J. ACM **48**(3), 407–430 (2001)

41. G. Manzini, Longest common prefix with mismatches, in *Proc. International Symposium on String Processing and Information Retrieval (SPIRE)*, pp. 299–310 (2015)

42. G. Manzini, P. Ferragina, Engineering a lightweight suffix array construction algorithm. Algorithmica **40**(1),33–50 (2004)

43. J.I. Munro, Tables, in *Proc. of Foundations of Software Technology and Theoretical Computer Science (FSTTCS)*, vol. 1180 of *LNCS*, pp. 37–42 (Springer, 1996)

44. J.I. Munro, G. Navarro, Y. Nekrich, Space-efficient construction of compressed indexes in deterministic linear time, in *Proc. ACM-SIAM Symposium on Discrete Algorithms (SODA)*, pp. 408–424 (2017)

45. S. Muthukrishnan, Efficient algorithms for document retrieval problems, in *Proc. ACM-SIAM Symposium on Discrete Algorithms (SODA)*, pp. 657–666 (2002)

46. G. Navarro, *Compact Data Structures: A Practical Approach* (Cambridge University Press, 2016)

47. G. Navarro, S.J. Puglisi, D. Valenzuela, Practical compressed document retrieval, in *Proc. Symposium on Experimental and Efficient Algorithms (SEA)*, pp. 193–205 (2011)

48. G. Nong, Practical linear-time O(1)-workspace suffix sorting for constant alphabets. ACM Trans. Inf. Syst. **31**(3), 1–15 (2013)

49. E. Ohlebusch, *Bioinformatics Algorithms: Sequence Analysis, Genome Rearrangements and Phylogenetic Reconstruction* (Oldenbusch Verlag, 2013)
50. E. Ohlebusch, S. Gog, Efficient algorithms for the all-pairs suffix-prefix problem and the all-pairs substring-prefix problem. Inf. Process. Lett. **110**(3), 123–128 (2010)
51. N. Prezza, G. Rosone, Space-efficient computation of the LCP array from the Burrows-Wheeler transform. CoRR (2019). abs/1901.05226
52. S.J. Puglisi, W.F. Smyth, A.H. Turpin, A taxonomy of suffix array construction algorithms. ACM Comput. Surv. **39**(2), 1–31 (2007)
53. K. Sadakane, Succinct representations of LCP information and improvements in the compressed suffix arrays, in *Proc. ACM-SIAM Symposium on Discrete Algorithms (SODA)*, pp. 225–232 (2002)
54. J. Seward, The bzip home page. http://www.bzip.org. Accessed: May, 2020
55. F. Shi, Suffix arrays for multiple strings: a method for on-line multiple string searches, in *Proc. Asian Computing Science Conference (ASIAN)*, pp. 11–22 (1996)
56. W.H.A. Tustumi, S. Gog, G.P. Telles, F.A. Louza, An improved algorithm for the all-pairs suffix-prefix problem. J. Discrete Algorithms **37**, 34–43 (2016)
57. N. Välimäki, V. Mäkinen, Space-efficient algorithms for document retrieval, in *Proc. Annual Symposium on Combinatorial Pattern Matching (CPM)*, pp. 205–215 (2007)
58. J. Vuillemin, A unifying look at data structures. Commun. ACM **23**(4), 229–239 (1980)
59. P. Weiner, Linear pattern matching algorithms, in *Proc. Annual Symposium on Switching and Automata Theory (SWAT)*, pp. 1–11 (1973)

Chapter 3
Induced Suffix Sorting

3.1 Introduction

Suffix sorting is one of the most important tasks in string processing. It is related to the construction of fundamental data structures that play a central role in bioinformatics, data compression, and combinatorics on words [32, 38, 45]. Given a string T with n symbols from an alphabet Σ of size σ, suffix sorting is the task of ordering all suffixes of T in lexicographical order. The resulting list of n integers denoting the starting positions of all sorted suffixes is the so-called *suffix array* [9, 33].

A naive approach for sorting all suffixes of T is to use a comparison-based algorithm, like merge-sort. This results in an $O(n^2 \log n)$ time solution [25], since each suffix comparison takes $O(n)$. Alternatively, the suffix array may be computed in $O(n)$ time by first building a suffix tree [56] and then obtaining the suffix order from its leaves [12]. Nonetheless, this approach is unfeasible in practice due to the large memory requirements of suffix trees.

Fortunately, by carefully arranging the computation of suffix relations, suffix sorting can be done in $O(n)$ time by specialized algorithms, and the suffix array can be computed directly, without resorting to suffix trees.

Several suffix sorting algorithms have been proposed since the introduction of the suffix array [14]. Puglisi et al. [49] and Dhaliwal et al. [5] present good reviews with more than 20 algorithms introduced in the past two decades. These algorithms were classified into three basic sorting techniques: prefix doubling, induced sorting, and recursion. To date, the fastest alternatives to compute the suffix array are based on induced sorting technique, where a small group of suffixes are sorted, and then used to deduce (induce) the order of the remaining suffixes. In Sect. 3.3 we review two remarkable suffix sorting algorithms, which are the basis of advances presented in Chaps. 4, 5, and 6.

© The Author(s), under exclusive licence to Springer Nature Switzerland AG 2020
F. A. Louza et al., *Construction of Fundamental Data Structures for Strings*,
SpringerBriefs in Computer Science, https://doi.org/10.1007/978-3-030-55108-7_3

Chronology:

1990:	Manber and Myers, in their seminal paper [33] that introduced the suffix array, also presented an $O(n \log n)$ time suffix sorting algorithm.
1997:	Farach [6] proposed a linear time suffix sorting algorithm to construct the suffix tree for integer alphabets.
2003:	Kim et al. [18], Kärkkäinen et al. [16] and Ko and Aluru [20] simultaneously presented the first linear time suffix array construction algorithms, all of them based on Farach's algorithm [6].
2009:	Nong et al. [42] presented a remarkable algorithm, called SAIS, the first linear time algorithm also fast in practice.
2013:	Nong [39] presented SACA-K, an improved variant of SAIS that runs in linear time using $\sigma + O(1)$ words of workspace, which is optimal for constant alphabets.
2018:	Li et al. [27] reduced the memory requirement of algorithm SACA-K to $O(1)$, removing the dependence on the alphabet size σ.

Fig. 3.1 Main landmarks in suffix sorting

3.2   A Brief History

In the early 1990s, in their seminal work Manber and Myers [33, 34] introduced the suffix array and presented an $O(n \log n)$ suffix sorting algorithm based on the *prefix-doubling* technique introduced earlier by Karp et al. [17]. Later, Sadakane [51] and Larsson [25] improved the practical performance of Manber and Myers's algorithm for real data inputs, and Itoh and Tanaka [13] and Seward [54] presented lightweight[1] algorithms that run in $O(n^2 \log n)$ time.

In 1994, Burrows and Wheeler [4] presented the so-called Burrows–Wheeler transform (BWT), which is based on a cyclic rotation of the list of all sorted suffixes. The BWT is the main component of popular lossless compression tools, like `bzip2` [53]. It is well-known that the BWT can be easily obtained from the suffix array, and vice versa. Therefore, the computation of suffix array and BWT are closely related problems.

In 2003, Kim et al. [19], Kärkkäinen et al. [16], and Ko and Aluru [21] independently presented the first linear time suffix array construction algorithms, all of them inspired in the recursive approach by Farach [6] to construct suffix trees [56]. However, although linear in the worst case, these algorithms were outperformed in practice by non-linear algorithms (e.g. [1, 48]). This happens because of the large constant factors hidden by the big O-notation, and due to the fact that for some application domains, the longest common prefix shared by suffixes of the same string is $O(\log n)$ [38], favoring non-linear alternatives. In 2006, Maniscalco and Puglisi [35] and Schurmann and Stoye [52] presented improved non-linear algorithms even faster in practice (see also Fig. 3.1).

---

[1]The term was coined by Manzini and Ferragina [36] to refer to algorithms with a small workspace.

In 2009, a remarkable suffix sorting algorithm, called SAIS, was introduced by Nong et al. [42]. SAIS builds heavily on induced sorting techniques by Ko and Aluru's [21] to compute the suffix array recursively in $O(n)$ time, being recognized as the first linear time suffix array construction algorithm that is also fast in practice. SAIS' practical behavior is stable on different inputs, while for non-linear algorithms there exist inputs for which they are not fast, typically repetitive strings. The workspace of SAIS is $0.5n + \sigma + O(1)$ words plus n bits for strings from constant alphabets [43, Corollary 3.14].

In 2013, Nong [39] introduced an elegant variant of algorithm SAIS, called SACA-K, introducing a clever memory usage strategy. The workspace of SACA-K is $\sigma + O(1)$ words, which is optimal for strings from constant alphabets. In practice, for ASCII texts, Nong's algorithm needs exactly n bytes plus $n + 256$ words of total memory. SACA-K runs in linear time and is fast in practice. More recently, Li et al. [27] and Goto [10] reduced the memory requirement of SACA-K to $O(1)$ words, which is independent of σ. In practice, for strings from integer alphabets, Li et al.'s algorithm needs overall $2n + O(1)$ words of memory, whereas SACA-K would need $3n + O(1)$ words. However, in that work [27] the authors have not compared their algorithm to previous implementations for integer alphabets (e.g. [26]).

The problem of computing the suffix array can essentially be considered solved [14], even though the development of faster practical algorithms is still an ongoing research area (e.g. [8, 47, 50, 55]).

It is noteworthy that, to date, the fastest suffix sorting implementation is an engineered variant of algorithm SAIS, called *divsufsort*, developed by Yuta Mori [37], which was not published by the author.

3.3 Induced Suffix Sorting

In this section we review algorithms SAIS [43] and SACA-K [39]. Our purpose is to provide the main ideas behind these algorithms and keep the presentation as simple as possible. Proofs and details may be found the original papers.

We define the *head* and the *tail* of c-buckets in the suffix array in addition to Definition 2.8, and we also define a counter array, referred to as bkt-array, to store head and tail values.

Definition 3.1 The *head* and the *tail* of a c-bucket refer to the first and to the last position of the c-bucket, respectively.

Definition 3.2 The bkt-array is an array of size σ that stores in bkt[c] the head (or the tail) of the c-bucket.

Throughout the algorithms, whenever a suffix position is inserted at the tail (or head) of a c-bucket in SA, the pointer bkt[c] is increased (or decreased) by one.

Induced suffix sorting was introduced by Itoh and Tanaka [13] and later refined by Ko and Aluru [20]. The suffixes are divided into groups, and the algorithm sorts

	1	2	3	4	5	6	7	8	9	10	11	12	13	14	15
T =	b	a	n	a	a	n	a	n	a	a	n	a	n	a	$
type =	L	S	L	S	S	L	S	L	S	S	L	S	L	L	S

Fig. 3.2 The types of each suffix in T = banaananaanana$. LMS-suffixes are highlighted in colors

the suffixes of one group, usually the smallest. Then, the order of remaining suffixes is computed (induced) from the sorted group.

3.3.1 SA in Linear Time

SAIS and SACA-K share the same divide-and-conquer framework. The algorithms differ in details that impact their workspace. In this section, we will refer to *IS algorithm* when describing common features of SAIS and SACA-K.

First, the suffixes are classified according to their lexicographic rank relative to their successor.

Definition 3.3 A suffix T_i is an *S-suffix* (stands for Smaller suffix) if $T_i < T_{i+1}$, otherwise T_i is an *L-suffix* (stands for Larger suffix). The last suffix, $T_n = \$$, is an S-suffix.

Remark 3.1 Within each c-bucket in $\mathsf{SA}[1, n]$, L-suffixes always precede S-suffixes.

The L/S classification can be performed in linear time by scanning $T[1, n]$ from right to left, for $i = n-1, n-2, \ldots, 1$. Starting with T_n as an S-suffix (by definition), T_i is set as an S-suffix if $T[i] < T[i+1]$ or $T[i] = T[i+1]$ and T_{i+1} is an S-suffix, otherwise T_i is set as an L-suffix.

SAIS precomputes the type of each suffix $T[i, n]$ and stores them in an additional bitvector **type** of size n, whereas SACA-K computes the type of each $T[i, n]$ on-the-fly in constant time (as we will see in Sect. 3.3.2).

Some suffixes are further classified as LMS-suffixes.

Definition 3.4 A suffix T_i is an *LMS-suffix* (stands for Left Most S-suffix) if T_i is an S-suffix and T_{i-1} is an L-suffix.

Example Figure 3.2 shows the suffix classification for the string $T =$ banaananaanana$.

SAIS uses array **type** to decide if T_i is an LMS-suffix, and SACA-K decides on-the-fly, in constant time, through the algorithm.

Steps:

1. Sort the LMS-suffixes and store in an auxiliary array SA^R.
2. Scan SA^R from right to left, $i = n^R, n^R - 1, \ldots, 1$, and insert each corresponding LMS-suffix of T into the tail of its c-bucket in SA.
3. Scan SA from left to right, $i = 1, 2, \ldots, n$, and for each suffix $T_{SA[i]}$, if $T_{SA[i]-1}$ is an L-suffix, insert $SA[i] - 1$ into the head of its bucket.
4. Scan SA from right to left, $i = n, n-1, \ldots, 1$, and for each suffix $T_{SA[i]}$, if $T_{SA[i]-1}$ is an S-suffix, insert $SA[i] - 1$ into the tail of its bucket.

Fig. 3.3 Induced sorting (IS)

The key observations of *IS algorithm* are that the order of the LMS-suffixes is enough to induce the order of all suffixes and that LMS-suffixes can also be recursively sorted in linear time.

IS algorithm (Fig. 3.3) works as follows. In Step 1, in order to sort the LMS-suffixes, $T[1, n]$ is divided into a set of substrings, called LMS-substrings.

Definition 3.5 An *LMS-substring* is a substring $T[i, j]$, where T_i and T_j are both LMS-suffixes, but no suffix starting in $T[i + 1, j - 1]$ is an LMS-suffix. The last suffix, $T_n = \$$, is an LMS-substring.

A modified version of *IS algorithm* is applied to sort all LMS-substrings. Starting from a modified Step 2', $T[1, n]$ is scanned, instead of $SA^R[1, n]$, and the starting position of each LMS-suffix is inserted at the tail of its c-bucket in SA. The operation of inserting a suffix at the head or tail of its c-bucket will be referred to as bucket sorting from this point on. Steps 3' and 4' are equal to Steps 3 and 4. At the end, all LMS-substrings are sorted and stored in their c-buckets [43, Theorem 3.12]. $SA[1, n]$ is scanned from left to right and the starting position of each LMS-substring is copied to the beginning of SA in the same order.

Example Figure 3.4 shows the sorting of all LMS-substrings following the algorithm above for the string $T = \texttt{banaananaanana\$}$. At the end of Step 4', the starting positions of all LMS-substrings are stored in order in $SA[1, n^R]$, where n^R is the number of LMS-substrings.

Let $s_1, s_2, \ldots, s_{n^R}$ be the LMS-substrings of T in order. A name r_i is assigned to each LMS-substring s_i of T. The naming procedures of SAIS and SACA-K differ. We will explain the approach adopted by SAIS in the next section.

3.3.1.1 Lexicographic Naming

Let σ^R be the number of distinct LMS-substrings of $T[1, n]$. SAIS assigns a *name* $r_i \in [1, \sigma^R]$ to each s_i such that $r_i < r_j$ if $s_i < s_j$ and $r_i = r_j$ if $s_i = s_j$. To do that,

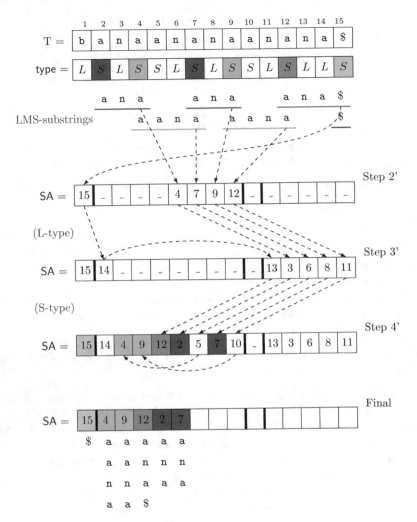

Fig. 3.4 Sorting all LMS-substrings with modified *IS algorithm* for $T =$ banaananaanana$. *c*-buckets in SA are separated by thicker vertical lines in the figure. Colors are used to help visually mapping suffixes through the algorithm. Colors will have the same meaning in the following figures as well

SA is scanned from left to right and each pair of consecutive LMS-substrings in SA is compared. LMS-substrings indexed by consecutive entries in $SA[1, n^R]$ may be equal, being assigned the same name. Names assigned to LMS-substrings may be seen as their rank. This procedure may be speed up by comparing their types and symbols [43].

A new reduced string $T^R = r_1 r_2 \dots r_{n^R}$ is created according to the names given to the LMS-substrings.

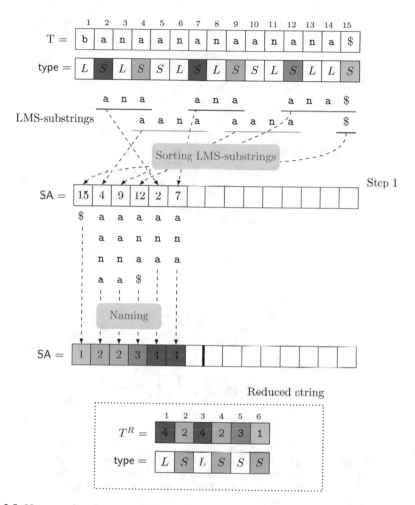

Fig. 3.5 Names assigned to each LMS-substring for $T = $ banaananaanana$ and the reduced string $T^R = $ 424231 as created by algorithm SAIS

Example Figure 3.5 shows the names assigned to each LMS-substring of $T = $ banaananaanana$, and the reduced string created by SAIS.

In the sequel, the suffix array of T^R, denoted as SA^R, is computed. If all LMS-substrings are distinct, $n^R = \sigma^R$, and SA^R is given as

$$\mathsf{SA}^R[T^R[i]] = i, \text{ for } i = 1, \ldots, n^R. \tag{3.1}$$

Otherwise, SAIS is applied recursively to sort all suffixes of T^R in SA^R. Note that the alphabet of T^R is integer, and T^R is also terminated by a unique smallest sentinel symbol that is smaller than any other symbol in $T^R[1, n^R - 1]$.

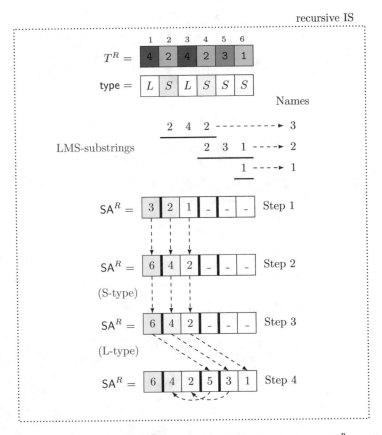

Fig. 3.6 Recursive call of SAIS for $T^R = 424231$. The LMS-substrings of T^R are all distinct and their names are 3, 2, 1 in text order. The suffix array for the next reduced string (namely $T^{R(2)}$) is given directly by Eq. 3.1 during Step 1. Then, Steps 2, 3, and 4 are performed and the final positions in SA^R give the suffix array of T^R. The algorithm is not invoked recursively again, and returns to the previous recursion level

Example Figure 3.6 shows the recursive call of SAIS for the reduced string $T^R = 424231$ created in Fig. 3.5.

An important remark is that the order of all LMS-suffixes in T can be determined by SA^R, that is, by the order of the respective suffixes in T^R.

In Step 2, the order of all LMS-suffixes is obtained from SA^R, which is stored in $SA[1, n^R]$. Note that, the length of T^R is at most $\lfloor n/2 \rfloor$, since there are at least three symbols in each LMS-substring, except for the last one, and two consecutive LMS-substrings overlap on a single symbol. Therefore, the space of $SA[n - n^R + 1, n]$ may be reused to temporarily store the inverse suffix array of T^R, denoted by ISA^R, which is used to decode suffix positions from T^R onto their corresponding LMS-suffixes in T. To do that, SA^R is scanned from left to right and ISA^R is computed as

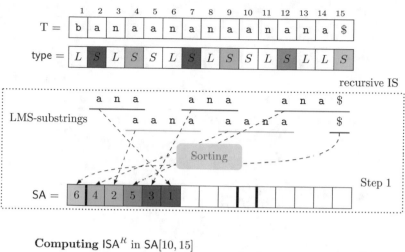

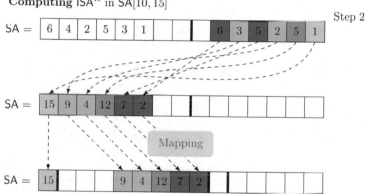

Fig. 3.7 Step 2 of *IS algorithm* for $T = \texttt{banaananaananas\$}$. ISA^R is temporarily stored in positions $\mathsf{SA}[10, 15]$. Then, each suffix of T^R is decoded into its corresponding positions in T. At the end, SA^R is scanned from right to left and suffixes are positioned into the tail of their c-buckets in $\mathsf{SA}[1, n]$

$$\mathsf{ISA}^R[\mathsf{SA}^R[i]] = i, \text{ for } i = 1, \ldots, n^R.$$

Then, both $T[1, n]$ and ISA^R are scanned from their last positions $i = n$ and $j = n^R$ to $i = 1$ and $j = 1$, respectively, such that for each LMS-suffix $T[i, n]$ the value in $\mathsf{SA}^R[\mathsf{ISA}^R[j]]$ receives i, decreasing j by one. At the end, the correct positions are stored in $\mathsf{SA}[1, n^R]$. Then, $\mathsf{SA}[1, n^R]$ is scanned and suffixes are inserted into the tail of their corresponding c-buckets in $\mathsf{SA}[1, n]$.

Example Figure 3.7 illustrates Step 2 of *IS algorithm* for the string $T = \texttt{banaananaananas\$}$.

In Step 3, the LMS-suffixes are already sorted and $\mathsf{SA}[1, n]$ is scanned from left to right, so that all L-suffixes are induced at their final, correct positions in SA.

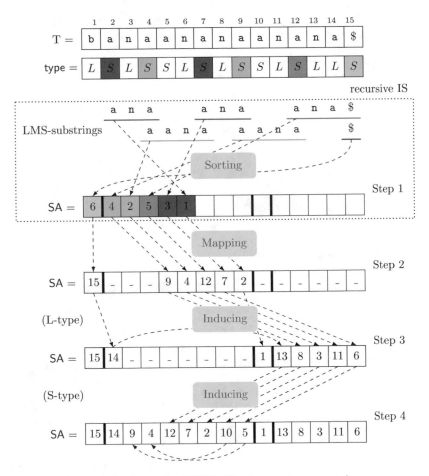

Fig. 3.8 Running example of algorithm SAIS for $T =$ banaananaanana$

In Step 4, all S-suffixes are induced from L-suffixes. This step is symmetric to Step 3. Therefore, at the end of Step 4 all suffixes are sorted and positioned in SA.

Example Figure 3.8 provides a complete running example of *IS algorithm* for the string $T =$ banaananaanana$. Steps 1 and 2 are further described in Figs. 3.4, 3.5, 3.6, and 3.7.

3.3.1.2   Reusing the Space of SA

Nong [39] observed that the space of $SA[1, n]$ is sufficient for storing both SA^R and T^R along all recursive calls of *IS algorithm*.

Problem Reduction

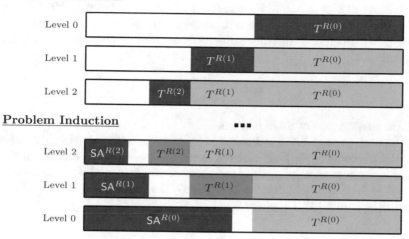

Problem Induction

Fig. 3.9 Reusing the space of SA[1, n] to store SA^R and T^R along all recursive calls of *IS algorithm*. At recursive level $l = k$, during the problem reduction the highlighted part (at the right) stores $T^{R(k)}$, whereas during problem induction the highlighted part (at the left) stores SA$^{R(k)}$. Figure adapted from [39, Fig. 2]

For a clearer presentation, to denote any structure used at recursive level l we add (l) to its symbol. That is, starting at level 0, SA$^{(l)}$ denotes the suffix array at level l, as well as for SA$^{R(l)}$, $T^{(l)}$, $T^{R(l)}$, $n^{(l)}$, and $n^{R(l)}$.

Note that, during the recursion, $T^{R(l)}$ and SA$^{R(l)}$ are $T^{(l+1)}$ and SA$^{(l+1)}$, respectively.

In order to reuse the space of SA[1, n] to store SA$^{R(l)}$ and $T^{R(l)}$ during recursive calls, a clever management of SA space is proposed. The key idea is that since the size of the reduced problem $n^{R(0)}$ is at most $\lfloor n^{(0)}/2 \rfloor$, it is possible to store at the right half part of SA$^{(0)}$ the reduced string T^R, leaving the left half unused. When *IS algorithm* is (recursively) called to sort the LMS-suffixes of $T^{R(0)}$, the left half of SA$^{(0)}$ is now taken as the whole space for SA$^{(1)}$, and so on through the recursion.

Suppose that the recursive calls terminate at level $l = k$. The space of SA corresponding to the rightmost $n/2, n/4, \ldots, n/2^k$ elements is used by the reduced strings, in the order $T^{R(0)}, T^{R(1)}, \ldots, T^{R(k)}$. Then, the first $n/2^k$ elements of SA are free, and the reduced suffix array SA$^{(k)}$ is computed and stored there. When the algorithm returns to the upper recursion level $l = k - 1$, SA$^{(k)}$ = SA$^{R(k-1)}$ is used to induce the suffixes of $T^{(k-1)}$ and construct SA$^{(k-1)}$, which is stored in the first $n/2^{k-1}$ elements of SA, overwriting SA$^{(k)}$, which may be discarded. This process continues until level 0 is reached, where SA$^{R(0)}$ will be stored in the left half part of SA, and SA$^{(0)}$ = SA will be constructed overwriting both SA$^{R(0)}$ and $T^{R(0)}$.

This way, the space of SA[1, n] is reused to store $T^{R(l)}$ and SA$^{R(l)}$, for all recursion levels.

Example Figure 3.9 illustrates this process, the highlighted parts of SA are occupied at the recursive level l.

Complexity Analysis
Steps 2, 3, and 4 of *IS algorithm* take linear time. In Step 1, the problem is reduced at least by half at each recursive call, since the size of the reduced string T^R is at most $\lfloor n/2 \rfloor$. Therefore, the time complexity is given by the following recurrence relation:

$$T(n) = T\left(\left\lfloor \frac{n}{2} \right\rfloor\right) + O(n)$$

and the running time of SAIS is $O(n)$.

The workspace of SAIS is dominated by the space needed to store the bkt-array and the bitvector type. Note that the space of bkt-array is no longer negligibly small across recursive calls, since the alphabet of T^R is integer, bounded by $n/2$. Therefore SAIS uses additional $0.5n + \sigma + O(1)$ words plus n bits for strings from constant alphabets [43, Corollary 3.14].

3.3.2 SA in Optimal Time and Space

In this section we show how to reduce the workspace of SAIS. The resulting algorithm, called SACA-K [39], runs in linear time using $\sigma + O(1)$ words of workspace, which is optimal for string from constant alphabets.

The two key observations of SACA-K are that the type of each suffix can be devised in constant time, and that the counter array bkt$[1, \sigma]$ is only necessary at recursion level 0, where the alphabet of T is σ.

3.3.2.1 Eliminating the type Array

The first novelty introduced by SACA-K is the elimination of the bitvector type$[1, n]$. It is only possible due to the way $T[1, n]$ is scanned through the algorithm. Recall that during Step 1 type is used to find the LMS-substrings, and during Steps 3 and 4 it is used to determine the type of $T_{\text{SA}[i]-1}$.

In Step 1 (when the LMS-substrings are sorted), the type of each suffix can be determined while $T[1, n]$ is scanned from right to left, as in the procedure described in Sect. 3.3.1. Then, whenever T_i is an S-suffix, the algorithm checks if the next scanned suffix T_{i-1} is an L-suffix. In this case, T_i is also an LMS-suffix and T_i is bucket sorted in SA according to its first symbol. However, in order to compare each consecutive LMS-substring for assigning their names, we have to know where each LMS-suffix ends. Fortunately, each LMS-substring has a type pattern governed by the regular expression S^+L^+S, which may be easily identified.

For example, suppose that a LMS-substring of T starts at $T[i]$. The symbols $T[i], T[i + 1], \ldots$ are traversed until reaching $T[e - 1] > T[e]$, for some $e > i$. Then $T_i, T_{i+1}, \ldots, T_{e-2}$ are S-suffixes. The symbols $T[e], T[e + 1], \ldots$ are traversed until reaching $T[k-1] < T[k]$, for some $k > e$. Then $T_{e-1}, T_e, \ldots T_{k-2}$ are L-suffixes and T_{k-1} is an S-suffix. Therefore, the LMS-substring starting at i ends at $k - 1$.

In Step 3 (when $\mathsf{SA}[1, n]$ is scanned from left to right and L-suffixes are induced), each scanned suffix already positioned in SA is either an LMS-suffix or an L-suffix. Then, it is enough to verify whether $T[\mathsf{SA}[i] - 1] \geq T[\mathsf{SA}[i]]$ to conclude that $T_{\mathsf{SA}[i]-1}$ is an L-suffix.

In Step 4 (when $\mathsf{SA}[1, n]$ is scanned from right to left, and S-suffixes are induced), $T_{\mathsf{SA}[i]-1}$ is an S-suffix if $T[\mathsf{SA}[i] - 1] < T[\mathsf{SA}[i]]$ or if $T[\mathsf{SA}[i]] = T[\mathsf{SA}[i]]$ and $\mathsf{bkt}[T[\mathsf{SA}[i-1]]] < i$. In other words, if $T_{\mathsf{SA}[i]}$ is an S-suffix, then $T_{\mathsf{SA}[i]-1}$ is also an S-suffix. Moreover, $T_{\mathsf{SA}[i]-1}$ is exactly the $(i-1)$-th smallest suffix of T that will be inserted into $\mathsf{SA}[i - 1] = \mathsf{bkt}[T[\mathsf{SA}[i - 1]]]$ in the corresponding iteration at Step 4.

3.3.2.2 Eliminating the bkt Array

The second and most notable improvement introduced by SACA-K is restricting the use of array $\mathsf{bkt}[1, \sigma]$ to the level $l = 0$ of the *IS algorithm*, which is an improvement since at each level $l > 0$ the alphabet of the reduced string $T^{R(l)}$ is integer, and the counter array $\mathsf{bkt}[1, \sigma^{R(l)}]$ is no longer negligibly small, as it is at level $l = 0$, where the alphabet size σ is constant.

The key idea is that, at level $l > 0$, the names assigned to LMS-substrings can be other than their lexicographical ranking (like in SAIS) as long as they maintain the same relative order. Therefore, the names are changed to index positions of SA, in such a way that for each L-suffix T_i^R the symbol $T^R[i] = r_i$ points to the head of its c-bucket in SA^R, and for each S-suffix T_j^R the symbol $T^R[j] = r_j$ points to the tail of its c-bucket in SA^R (see [39, Property 4.1]). Recall that the alphabet of $T^{R(l)}$ is integer, which allows storing integer values.

Example Figure 3.10 shows the naming produced by SACA-K for the LMS-substrings of $T = \mathsf{banaananaaanana\$}$. For example, $T^R[2] < T^R[1]$ and their ranks are 2 and 4.

Note that the relative order between all LMS-substrings is maintained, since given any two symbols $r_i < r_j$ named by SAIS the equivalent names given by SACA-K will have the same relative order, since $\mathsf{bkt}[r_i] < \mathsf{bkt}[r_j]$. When $r_i = r_j$ during SAIS naming, if both r_i and r_j are of the same type (either S-suffixes or L-suffixes), they will be given the same name by SACA-K. However if they are of different types, the L-suffix will receive a smaller name than that of the S-suffix, but this does not change the relative order of the suffixes in $T^{R(l)}$, since L-suffixes are always smaller than S-suffixes.

Therefore, in Steps 2–4, whenever a suffix $T_i^{(l)}$ has to be inserted into its bucket, the value stored in $T^{(l)}[i]$ points to the head (or to the tail) of its c-bucket. Such position in $\mathsf{SA}^{(l)}$ is reserved to indicate how many suffixes of that bucket had already been added. That is, if a c-bucket starting in $\mathsf{SA}^{(l)}[j]$ has already received k suffixes,

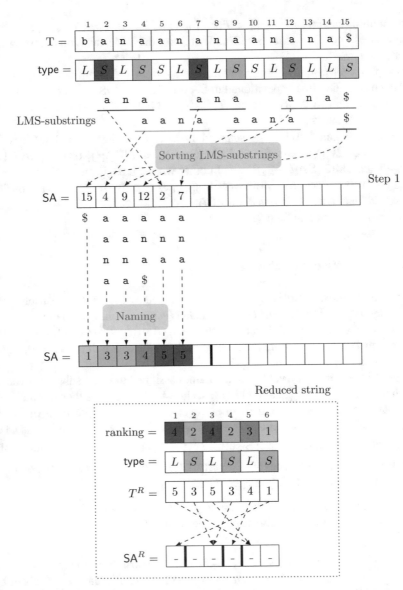

Fig. 3.10 Naming procedure of SACA-K for the LMS-substrings of $T =$ banaananaanana$, creating the reduced string $T^R =$ 535341. The figure also shows the rank of each LMS-substring, in text order

then $\mathsf{SA}^{(l)}[j] = k$. Thus, whenever a suffix $T_i^{(l)}$ is inserted into its bucket, the value in $\mathsf{SA}^{(l)}[T^{(l)}[i]]$ is incremented (or decremented) by one position, and $T_i^{(l)}$ is inserted into the position pointed by $\mathsf{SA}^{(l)}[T^{(l)}[i]]$. When a c-bucket gets full, all its suffixes are shifted one position to the left (or to the right).

Finally, in order to know whether a bucket is full, it is necessary to find out if the position to which $SA^{(l)}[j]$ points to is a bucket start. SACA-K takes advantage of the fact that at level $l > 0$ the most significant bit of any element in SA is available, since the reduced problem size is at most $n/2$. Thus, if $SA^{(l)}[j]$ points to a bucket start, its most significant bit is set to 1. We may say that $SA^{(l)}[j]$ stores a negative integer value if it is a bucket start.

Complexity Analysis

The running time of SACA-K is $O(n)$, since all improvements maintain SAIS time complexity [39, Section 5.1].

The workspace of SACA-K is dominated by the space used by the bkt-array, which is needed only at the top recursive level $l = 0$, when it has size σ. Therefore, SACA-K uses additional $\sigma + O(1)$ words of workspace, which is optimal for strings from constant alphabets.

The overall memory space required by SACA-K for constant alphabets is n bytes plus n words (for the input $T[1, n]$ and output $SA[1, n]$) and $\sigma + O(1)$ words of workspace.

3.4 Concluding Remarks

Since the introduction of the algorithms SAIS and SACA-K, different alternatives have been proposed to adapt them to external memory (e.g. [3, 15, 28, 40, 41, 57]) and to parallel architectures (e.g. [22–24, 58]).

There are also solutions that adapt SAIS and SACA-K to compute additional data structures as a by-product of the suffix array construction, the so-called augmented suffix sorting (e.g. [2, 7, 8, 11, 29–31, 44, 46]).

In Part II of this book we present three different augmented algorithms that modify SACA-K to compute together with the suffix array, the longest common prefix array (Chap. 4), the document array (Chap. 5), and the Lyndon array (Chap. 6). These algorithms are optimal in time and space for strings from constant alphabets, and represent theoretical and practical advances in the construction of these data structures.

References

1. A. Antonitio, P.J. Ryan, W.F. Smyth, A. Turpin, X. Yu, New suffix array algorithms - linear but not fast? in *Proc. Australasian Workshop on Combinatorial Algorithms (AWOCA)*, pp. 148–156 (2004)
2. T. Beller, M. Zwerger, S. Gog, E. Ohlebusch, Space-efficient construction of the Burrows-Wheeler transform, in *Proc. International Symposium on String Processing and Information Retrieval (SPIRE)*, pp. 5–16 (Springer International Publishing, 2013)

3. T. Bingmann, J. Fischer, V. Osipov, Inducing suffix and LCP arrays in external memory. J. Exp. Algorithmics **21**(2), 2.3:1–2.3:27 (2016)
4. M. Burrows, D.J. Wheeler, A block-sorting lossless data compression algorithm. Technical report, Digital SRC Research Report, 1994
5. J. Dhaliwal, S.J. Puglisi, A. Turpin,   Trends in suffix sorting: a survey of low memory algorithms, in *Proc. Australasian Computer Science Conference (ACSC)*, pp. 91–98 (2012)
6. M. Farach, Optimal suffix tree construction with large alphabets, in *Proc. Annual IEEE Symposium on Foundations of Computer Science (FOCS)*, pp. 137–143 (1997)
7. J. Fischer, Inducing the LCP-array, in *Proc. Workshop on Algorithms and Data Structures (WADS)*, pp. ges 374–385 (2011)
8. J. Fischer, F. Kurpicz, Dismantling divsufsort, in *Proc. Prague Stringology Conference (PSC)*, pp. 62–76 (2017)
9. G.H. Gonnet, R.A. Baeza-Yates, T. Snider, New indices for text: PAT trees and PAT arrays, in *Information Retrieval*, pp. 66–82 (Prentice-Hall, 1992)
10. K. Goto, Optimal time and space construction of suffix arrays and LCP arrays for integer alphabets, in *Proc. Prague Stringology Conference (PSC)*, pp. 111–125 (2019)
11. K. Goto, H. Bannai, Space efficient linear time Lempel-Ziv factorization for small alphabets, in *Proc. IEEE Data Compression Conference (DCC)*, pp. 163–172 (2014)
12. D. Gusfield, *Algorithms on Strings, Trees and Sequences: Computer Science and Computational Biology* (Cambridge University Press, 1997)
13. H. Itoh, H. Tanaka, An efficient method for in memory construction of suffix arrays, in *Proc. International Symposium on String Processing and Information Retrieval (SPIRE)*, pp. 81–88 (1999)
14. J. Kärkkäinen, Suffix array construction, in *Encyclopedia of Algorithms*, pp. 2141–2144 (Springer, 2016)
15. J. Kärkkäinen, D. Kempa, S.J. Puglisi, B. Zhukova, Engineering external memory induced suffix sorting, in *Proc. Workshop on Algorithm Engineering and Experimentation (ALENEX)*, pp. 98–108 (2017)
16. J. Kärkkäinen, P. Sanders, S. Burkhardt, Simple linear work suffix array construction, in *Proc. International Colloquium on Automata, Languages and Programming (ICALP)*, pp. 943–955 (2003)
17. R.M. Karp, R.E. Miller, A.L. Rosenberg, Rapid identification of repeated patterns in strings, trees and arrays, in *Proc. of the 4th Annual ACM Symposium on Theory of Computing, May 1–3, 1972, Denver, Colorado, USA*, pp. 125–136 (1972)
18. D.K. Kim, J.S. Sim, H. Park, K. Park, Linear-time construction of suffix arrays, in *Proc. Annual Symposium on Combinatorial Pattern Matching (CPM)*, pp. 186–199 (2003)
19. D.K. Kim, J.S. Sim, H. Park, K. Park, Constructing suffix arrays in linear time. J. Discrete Algorithms **3**(2–4), 126–142 (2005)
20. P. Ko, S. Aluru, Space efficient linear time construction of suffix arrays, in *Proc. Annual Symposium on Combinatorial Pattern Matching (CPM)*, pp. 200–210 (2003)
21. P. Ko, S. Aluru, Space efficient linear time construction of suffix arrays. J. Discrete Algorithms **3**(2–4), 143–156 (2005)
22. J. Labeit, J. Shun, G.E. Blelloch, Parallel lightweight wavelet tree, suffix array and FM-index construction. J. Discrete Algorithms **43**, 2–17 (2017)
23. B. Lao, G. Nong, W.H. Chan, Y. Pan, Fast induced sorting suffixes on a multicore machine. J. Supercomput. **74**(7), 3468–3485 (2018)
24. B. Lao, G. Nong, W.H. Chan, J.Y. Xie, Fast in-place suffix sorting on a multicore computer. IEEE Trans. Comput. **67**(12), 1737–1749 (2018)
25. N.J. Larsson, Notes on suffix sorting. Technical report, LU-CS-TR, Lund University, Sweden, 1998
26. N.J. Larsson, K. Sadakane, Faster suffix sorting. Theor. Comput. Sci. **387**, 258–272 (2007)
27. Z. Li, J. Li, H. Huo, Optimal in-place suffix sorting, in *Proc. International Symposium on String Processing and Information Retrieval (SPIRE)*, pp. 268–284 (2018)

28. W.J. Liu, G. Nong, W.H. Chan, Y. Wu, Induced sorting suffixes in external memory with better design and less space, in *Proc. International Symposium on String Processing and Information Retrieval (SPIRE)*, pp. 83–94 (2015)

29. F.A. Louza, S. Gog, G.P. Telles, Inducing enhanced suffix arrays for string collections. Theor. Comput. Sci. **678**, 22–39 (2017)

30. F.A. Louza, S. Gog, G.P. Telles, Optimal suffix sorting and LCP array construction for constant alphabets. Inf. Process. Lett. **118**, 30–34 (2017)

31. F.A. Louza, S. Mantaci, G. Manzini, M. Sciortino, G.P. Telles, Inducing the Lyndon array, in *Proc. International Symposium on String Processing and Information Retrieval (SPIRE)*, pp. 138–151 (2019)

32. V. Mäkinen, D. Belazzougui, F. Cunial, A.I. Tomescu, *Genome-Scale Algorithm Design* (Cambridge University Press, 2015)

33. U. Manber, G. Myers, Suffix arrays: a new method for on-line string searches, in *Proc. ACM-SIAM Symposium on Discrete Algorithms (SODA)*, pp. 319–327 (1990)

34. U. Manber, G. Myers, Suffix arrays: a new method for on-line string searches. SIAM J. Comput. **22**(5), 935–948 (1993)

35. M.A. Maniscalco, S.J. Puglisi, Faster lightweight suffix array construction, in *Proc. Australasian Workshop on Combinatorial Algorithms (AWOCA)*, pp. 122–133 (2006)

36. G. Manzini, P. Ferragina, Engineering a lightweight suffix array construction algorithm. Algorithmica **40**(1), 33–50 (2004)

37. Y. Mori, divsufsort. https://github.com/y-256/libdivsufsort

38. G. Navarro, *Compact Data Structures: A Practical Approach* (Cambridge University Press, 2016)

39. G. Nong, Practical linear-time O(1)-workspace suffix sorting for constant alphabets. ACM Trans. Inf. Syst. **31**(3), 1–15 (2013)

40. G. Nong, W.H. Chan, S.Q. Hu, Y. Wu, Induced sorting suffixes in external memory. ACM Trans. Inf. Syst. **33**(3), 12:1–12:15 (2015)

41. G. Nong, W.H. Chan, S. Zhang, X.F. Guan, Suffix array construction in external memory using d-critical substrings. ACM Trans. Inf. Syst. **32**, 1:1–1:15 (2014)

42. G. Nong, S. Zhang, W.H. Chan, Linear suffix array construction by almost pure induced-sorting, in *Proc. IEEE Data Compression Conference (DCC)*, pp. 193–202 (2009)

43. G. Nong, S. Zhang, W.H. Chan, Two efficient algorithms for linear time suffix array construction. IEEE Trans. Comput. **60**(10), 1471–1484 (2011)

44. D.S.N. Nunes, F.A. Louza, S. Gog, M. Ayala-Rincón, G. Navarro, A grammar compression algorithm based on induced suffix sorting, in *Proc. IEEE Data Compression Conference (DCC)*, pp. 42–51 (2018)

45. E. Ohlebusch, *Bioinformatics Algorithms: Sequence Analysis, Genome Rearrangements and Phylogenetic Reconstruction* (Oldenbusch Verlag, 2013)

46. D. Okanohara, K. Sadakane, A linear-time Burrows-Wheeler transform using induced sorting, in *Proc. International Symposium on String Processing and Information Retrieval (SPIRE)*, vol. 5721 of *LNCS*, pp. 90–101 (Springer, 2009)

47. Z. Peng, Y. Wang, X. Xue, J. Wei, An efficient algorithm for suffix sorting. Int. J. Pattern Recognit. Artif. Intell. **30**(6), 1659018 (2016)

48. S.J. Puglisi, W.F. Smyth, A. Turpin, The performance of linear time suffix sorting algorithms, in *Proc. IEEE Data Compression Conference (DCC)*, pp. 358–367 (2005)

49. S.J. Puglisi, W.F. Smyth, A.H. Turpin, A taxonomy of suffix array construction algorithms. ACM Comput. Surv. **39**(2), 1–31 (2007)

50. S. Rajasekaran, M. Nicolae, An elegant algorithm for the construction of suffix arrays. J. Discrete Algorithms **27**, 21–28 (2014)

51. K. Sadakane, A fast algorithm for making suffix arrays and for Burrows-Wheeler transformation, in *Proc. IEEE Data Compression Conference (DCC)*, pp. 129–138 (1998)

52. K.-B. Schürmann, J. Stoye, An incomplex algorithm for fast suffix array construction. Softw. Pract. Exp. **37**(3), 309–329 (2007)

53. J. Seward, The bzip home page. http://www.bzip.org. Accessed: May, 2020

54. J. Seward, On the performance of BWT sorting algorithms, in *Proc. IEEE Data Compression Conference (DCC)*, pp. 173–182 (2000)
55. N. Timoshevskaya, W.C. Feng, SAIS-OPT: on the characterization and optimization of the SA-IS algorithm for suffix array construction, in *Proc. International Conference on Computational Advances in Bio and Medical Sciences (ICCABS)*, pp. 1–6 (2014)
56. P. Weiner, Linear pattern matching algorithms, in *Proc. Annual Symposium on Switching and Automata Theory (SWAT)*, pp. 1–11 (1973)
57. Y. Wu, B. Lao, X. Ma, G. Nong, An improved algorithm for building suffix array in external memory, in *Proc. International Symposium on Parallel Architectures, Algorithms and Programming (PAAP)*, pp. 320–330 (2019)
58. J.Y. Xie, B. Lao, G. Nong, In-place suffix sorting on a multicore computer with better design, in *Proc. International Symposium on Parallel Architectures, Algorithms and Programming (PAAP)*, pp. 331–342 (2019)

Part II
Augmented Suffix Sorting

Chapter 4
Inducing the LCP Array

4.1 Introduction

The *longest common prefix* (LCP) array is a versatile data structure that provides the length of the longest common prefix between consecutive suffixes in the suffix array. The LCP array was introduced by Manber and Myers [19], by the name of Hgt-array, as an additional data structure to speed up string matching algorithms over the suffix array.

In 2004, Abouelhoda et al. [2] showed that the combination of the suffix array and the LCP array (known as enhanced suffix array) can be used for simulating algorithms that required suffix tree [31] navigation with the same asymptotic complexity while using much less memory space in practice [3]. Since then, a particular emphasis has been put on compact alternatives to suffix trees and several variations of such indexes have been proposed in which the LCP array is one of the main components (e.g. [1, 6, 7, 11, 12, 14, 21–23, 26, 29, 30]).

The LCP array can be computed in linear time from the already computed suffix array. In 2001, Kasai et al. [16] introduced the first algorithm of this kind, which has been further improved by Manzini [20] and by Kärkkäinen et al. [15]. The LCP array can be also computed in linear time from the Burrows–Wheeler transform (BWT) [5] with a small practical slowdown while using much less memory [4, 28]. To date, however, the fastest known alternative is to compute

---

This chapter is based on [18]. It was first published in: *Information Processing Letters* (v. 118) and republished here with the permission of the copyright holder.

© The Author(s), under exclusive licence to Springer Nature Switzerland AG 2020
F. A. Louza et al., *Construction of Fundamental Data Structures for Strings*,
SpringerBriefs in Computer Science, https://doi.org/10.1007/978-3-030-55108-7_4

the LCP array during the suffix array construction, as a by-product of algorithms
SAIS [25] and SACA-K [24] (described in Chap. 3).

In this chapter we present a variant of algorithm SACA-K that also computes
the LCP array. This augmented algorithm, introduced by Louza et al. [17], runs in
$O(n\sigma)$ time using $4\sigma + O(1)$ words of workspace, which is optimal for strings from
constant alphabets. We present experiments that show a competitive performance
and that evaluate the overhead added by the LCP array computation.

4.2   Inducing the LCP Array

In this section we show how to modify algorithm SACA-K to also compute the LCP
array, referred to as SACA-K+LCP [17]. It is noteworthy that SACA-K+LCP adapts
Fischer's [8] ideas proposed to compute the LCP array during algorithm SAIS.

We first recall the main steps of SACA-K (the same of *IS algorithm*, presented in
Sect. 3.3.1 and shown again in Fig. 4.1).

Also, recall that whenever a suffix position is inserted at the tail (or head) of a
c-bucket in SA, the pointer bkt[c] is increased (or decreased) by one.

Example Figure 4.2 shows a running example of algorithm SACA-K for the string
$T = $ banaananaanana\$ (also presented in Sect. 3.3.1).

The key observation to adapt SACA-K is that the LCP values between consecutive entries in SA can also be induced during Steps 3 and 4 (at the top recursion
level) given a partial LCP array between LMS-suffixes, which can be computed in
linear time in Step 1.

Steps:

1. Sort the LMS-suffixes and store in an auxiliary array SA^R.

2. Scan SA^R from right to left, $i = n^R, n^R - 1, \ldots, 1$, and insert each corresponding LMS-suffix of T into the tail of its c-bucket in SA.

3. Scan SA from left to right, $i = 1, 2, \ldots, n$, and for each suffix $T_{SA[i]}$, if
   $T_{SA[i]-1}$ is an L-suffix, insert $SA[i] - 1$ into the head of its bucket.

4. Scan SA from right to left , $i = n, n - 1, \ldots, 1$, and for each suffix $T_{SA[i]}$, if
   $T_{SA[i]-1}$ is an S-suffix, insert $SA[i] - 1$ into the tail of its bucket.

Fig. 4.1 *IS algorithm*

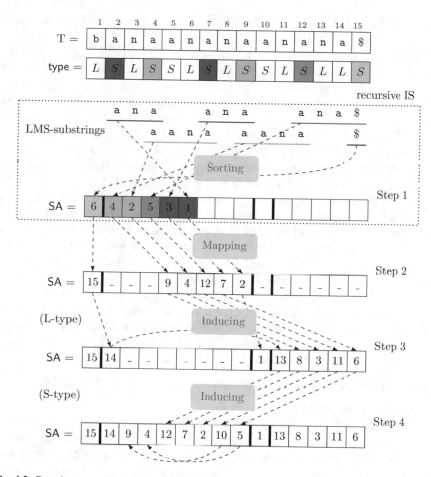

Fig. 4.2 Running example of algorithm SACA-K for $T = $ banaananaanana$ (refer to Sect. 3.3.1 for further examples)

4.2.1 LCP Array in Linear Time

First, we explain how to modify Steps 3 and 4 to induce LCP values. The explanation of Steps 1 and 2 will be postponed until the end of this section.

Let us assume that the LCP values between every consecutive LMS-suffix positioned in $\mathsf{SA}[1, n]$ at the end of Step 2 have been computed and are given at their corresponding positions in $\mathsf{LCP}[1, n]$.

In Step 3, whenever two L-suffixes $T_{\mathsf{SA}[j]-1}$ and $T_{\mathsf{SA}[i]-1}$ are positioned (induced) at adjacent $\mathsf{SA}[k - 1]$ and $\mathsf{SA}[k]$, the value of $\mathsf{LCP}[k] = \mathsf{lcp}(T_{\mathsf{SA}[j]-1}, T_{\mathsf{SA}[i]-1})$ can be computed by the lcp between their succeeding suffixes $T_{\mathsf{SA}[j]}$ and $T_{\mathsf{SA}[i]}$, which are already sorted in $\mathsf{SA}[1, i]$, by the order in which the suffixes are induced and positioned in SA, that is, $1 \leq j < i < k \leq n$.

Then, $\mathsf{lcp}(T_{\mathsf{SA}[j]}, T_{\mathsf{SA}[i]})$ is given by a range minimum query (rmq) over the partial LCP array computed up to iteration i as follows.

Given that suffixes from positions j and i induce $T_{\mathsf{SA}[j]-1}$ and $T_{\mathsf{SA}[i]-1}$ at $\mathsf{SA}[k-1]$ and $\mathsf{SA}[k]$, respectively, where $j < i < k$. We have one of the following cases. If k is the first position of a c-bucket, then $\mathsf{LCP}[k] = 0$. Otherwise, $T[\mathsf{SA}[j] - 1]$ and $T[\mathsf{SA}[i] - 1]$ are equal, and $T_{\mathsf{SA}[i]-1}$ and $T_{\mathsf{SA}[j]-1}$ are in the same c-bucket. In this case, if j and i are positions in different c-buckets, then $T[\mathsf{SA}[j]] \neq T[\mathsf{SA}[i]]$ and $\mathsf{LCP}[k] = 1$, otherwise, $\mathsf{LCP}[k] = \mathsf{lcp}(T_{\mathsf{SA}[j]}, T_{\mathsf{SA}[i]}) + 1$. The value of $\mathsf{lcp}(T_{\mathsf{SA}[j]}, T_{\mathsf{SA}[i]})$ is given by the $\mathsf{rmq}(i, j)$, as detailed in Sect. 2.2.2.

A particular case happens whenever $T_{\mathsf{SA}[j]}$ is L-type and $T_{\mathsf{SA}[i]}$ is S-type, then $\mathsf{lcp}(T_{\mathsf{SA}[j]}, T_{\mathsf{SA}[i]}) = 1$ since $T[\mathsf{SA}[j] + 1] \neq T[\mathsf{SA}[i] + 1]$.

There exist different alternatives to compute $\mathsf{rmq}(i, j)$, which may impact in the overall running time and workspace of the algorithm. The *simplest one* scans the interval $\mathsf{LCP}[i + 1, j]$ for each rmq evaluation, increasing the running time to $O(n^2)$. The *second alternative* is to keep an auxiliary array C of length σ up-to-date, such that, at each iteration $i = 1, 2, \ldots, n$, $\mathsf{C}[c]$ gives the minimum LCP value between the current suffix $T_{\mathsf{SA}[i]}$ and the last suffix $T_{\mathsf{SA}[j]}$ that have induced a suffix starting with symbol c. Then, at each iteration i, an $O(\sigma)$ time procedure is needed to update all values of $\mathsf{C}[1, \sigma]$. This alternative increases the running time to $O(n\sigma)$ and adds σ words to the workspace. Finally, a *third alternative* is to use a *semi-dynamic* rmq data structure [9] to solve each rmq in $O(1)$ time adding $2n + o(n)$ bits to the workspace.

Example Figure 4.3 illustrates iterations $i = 1, 2, \ldots, 6$ of the modified Step 3.

Step 4 is symmetric to Step 3.

At the end of Step 4, the LCP values between the last L-suffix and the first S-suffix of each c-bucket are computed by direct comparison, since they are not induced in the same step of the algorithm. Fortunately, the LCP value between such suffixes can only involve equal symbols, allowing us to easily compute them in linear time [8, Lemma 3].

Example Figure 4.4 shows a complete running example of SACA-K+LCP for the string $T = \mathtt{banaananaanana\$}$.

We now discuss how to modify Step 1 to compute the LCP values between every consecutive LMS-suffix in $\mathsf{SA}[1, n^R]$, denoted by $\mathsf{LCP}^{\mathsf{LMS}}$.

There are two possible approaches. The first one is to compute the LCP array for the reduced string T^R, denoted by LCP^R, together with SA^R recursively, and then derive $\mathsf{LCP}^{\mathsf{LMS}}$ into $\mathsf{LCP}[1, n^R]$ at the end of Step 1. Note that at the bottom recursion level l (see Sect. 3.3.1.2), when the LMS-substrings of $T^{R(l)}$ are all distinct, $\mathsf{SA}^{R(l)}$ is given directly by Eq. 3.1 and $\mathsf{LCP}^{R(l)}$ has all values equal to zero. The problem is that the values in LCP^R refer to symbols in T^R, which correspond to LMS-substrings in T. Then, whenever a recursive call returns $\mathsf{SA}^{R(l)}$ and $\mathsf{LCP}^{R(l)}$, the LCP values have to be "scaled-up" by the lengths of the corresponding LMS-substrings in $T^{(l)}$ to obtain $\mathsf{LCP}^{\mathsf{LMS}(l)}$, which can be done in

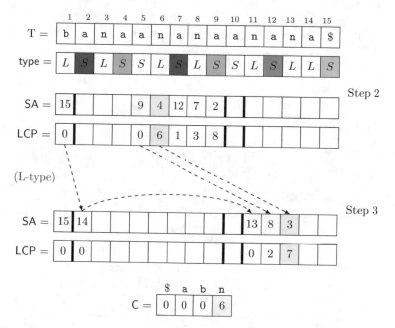

Fig. 4.3 Computing LCP values in Step 3 (iterations $i = 1, 2, \ldots, 6$) for $T = $ banaananaananas. At iterations $i = 1$ and $i = 2$ suffixes T_{14} and T_{13} are induced at the first position of their c-buckets, and, therefore, LCP[2] = 0 and LCP[11] = 0. At iteration $i = 5$, suffix T_8 is induced by an L-suffix at position $k = 12$, while T_{13} was induced by an S-suffix at position $k - 1 = 11$, both from the same c-bucket. In this case, LCP[12] = lcp$(T_{14}, T_9) + 1 = 1 + 1 = 2$. At iteration $i = 6$, T_3 is induced by a suffix from the same c-bucket of T_9, in this case LCP[13] = lcp$(T_9, T_4) + 1 = 7$. Then, lcp$(T_9, T_4) = $ rmq$(5, 6) = 6$ is computed using array $C[1, \sigma]$ illustrated at the bottom of the figure. Colors are used to help visually mapping suffixes through the algorithm. Colors will have the same meaning in the following figures as well

linear time using $n^{R(l)}$ additional words to store the lengths of each LMS-substring at level l (see [8, Section 3.3]). In the worst case, however, n words are added to the overall workspace.

The other, simpler approach to obtain LCP^{LMS} is to compute it immediately at the end of Step 1 (only at the top recursion level) when the LMS-suffixes are given sorted in SA[1, n^R]. We can use a sparse variant of any LCP array construction algorithm (e.g. [15, 16, 20]) to compare suffixes in $T^{(0)}[1, n]$. This can be done in linear time using $n^{R(0)}$ words to store the sparse set (positions) of sorted suffixes. In the worst case, it adds $n/2$ words to the overall workspace.

In Step 2, the LCP values in LCP^{LMS} are stored in their corresponding positions in LCP[1, n^R]. These values are mapped into the c-buckets in the same way the SA entries are positioned.

Complexity Analysis

The running time and workspace of the algorithm depend on the alternatives chosen for Steps 1, 3, and 4. Note that when LCP^{LMS} is obtained through LCP^R (computed

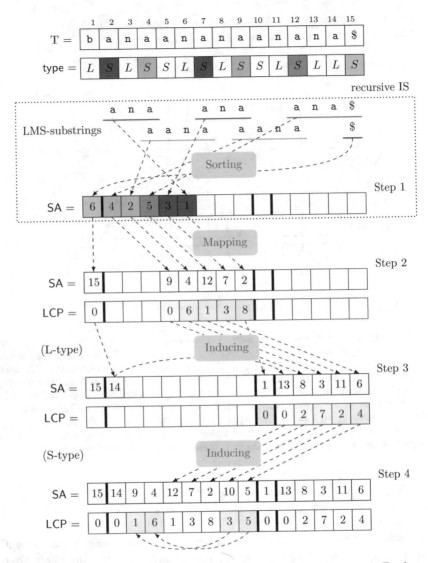

Fig. 4.4 Running example of SACA-K+LCP for $T =$ banaananaanana\$. For instance, suffixes T_{14} and T_9 have their symbols directly compared to compute LCP[3] $= 1$ since T_{14} is the last L-suffix and T_9 is the first S-suffix of c-bucket

recursively) in Step 1, the running time of the second alternative to compute rmq in Steps 3 and 4 becomes $O(n^2)$, since the alphabet size σ^R is no longer constant in recursive calls. On the other hand, if we choose the third alternative for rmq, the workspace is increased to $2n + o(n)$ bits.

Then, given the second approach that computes LCP^{LMS} in linear time immediately at the end of Step 1 at the top recursion level, combined with the second alternative that computes each rmq in $O(\sigma)$ time during Steps 3 and 4, the resulting algorithm runs in $O(n\sigma)$ time and needs $0.5n + \sigma + O(1)$ extra words on top of what is needed to compute the suffix array.

Fischer [8] implemented a variant of SAIS, referred to as SAIS+LCP, that applies the above combination of approaches to compute the suffix array together with LCP array in $O(n\sigma)$ time using $n + 2\sigma + O(1)$ words plus n bits of workspace, which is linear for strings from constant alphabets.

4.2.2 LCP Array in Optimal Time and Space

In this section we show how to reduce the workspace of the algorithm to $\sigma + O(1)$ words, which is optimal for strings from constant alphabets.

The key idea is to reuse the space of $\mathsf{SA}[n - n^R + 1, n]$ and $\mathsf{LCP}[1, n]$ to store auxiliary arrays needed to compute $\mathsf{LCP}^{\mathsf{LMS}}$ immediately at the end of Step 1. Moreover, we can speed up the computation of $\mathsf{LCP}^{\mathsf{LMS}}$ when LMS-substrings are compared during *naming* procedure.

We use a sparse variant of the $\varPhi$-algorithm [15] that computes the PLCP array in linear time, then we derive $\mathsf{LCP}^{\mathsf{LMS}}$. The original $\varPhi$-algorithm requires $2n^R$ extra words to store $\varPhi$ and PLCP arrays. Additionally, we need an array RA to store the n^R text positions of the LMS-suffixes to be considered by the sparse algorithm. We will see how to store $\varPhi$, RA, and PLCP arrays into $\mathsf{SA}[n-n^R+1, n]$ and $\mathsf{LCP}[1, n]$, and then obtain $\mathsf{LCP}^{\mathsf{LMS}}$ in $\mathsf{LCP}[1, n^R]$ in linear time.

First, we show how to precompute LCP values during Step 1. Note that when consecutive LMS-substrings (sorted and positioned in $\mathsf{SA}[1, n^R]$) are compared one-by-one to compute their ranks (*naming* procedure), we can obtain the lcp between them as a by-product of their symbol comparisons with no additional costs. These LCP values can speed up the computation of $\mathsf{LCP}^{\mathsf{LMS}}$, since any two consecutive LMS-suffixes in positions $\mathsf{SA}[i]$ and $\mathsf{SA}[i+1]$ may share a prefix larger or equal to the LCP value between their (initial) LMS-substrings. We store this partial $\mathsf{LCP}^{\mathsf{LMS}}$ in the first half of array $\mathsf{LCP}[1, n]$, that is, $\mathsf{LCP}[1, n^R]$.

Example Figure 4.5 shows an example where the LCP values between the LMS-substrings are precomputed during *naming* procedure and stored in $\mathsf{LCP}[1, 6]$.

When the recursive call of Step 1 returns SA^R, stored in $\mathsf{SA}[1, n^R]$, we map the precomputed values in $\mathsf{LCP}[1, n^R]$ into the permuted LCP array, named $\mathsf{PLCP}^{\mathsf{LMS}}$, stored in the second half of LCP, that is, $\mathsf{LCP}[n - n^R + 1, n]$. Recall that there are at most $n/2$ LMS-suffixes, so $\mathsf{LCP}^{\mathsf{LMS}}$ and $\mathsf{PLCP}^{\mathsf{LMS}}$ do not overlap. This partial $\mathsf{PLCP}^{\mathsf{LMS}}$ is obtained as

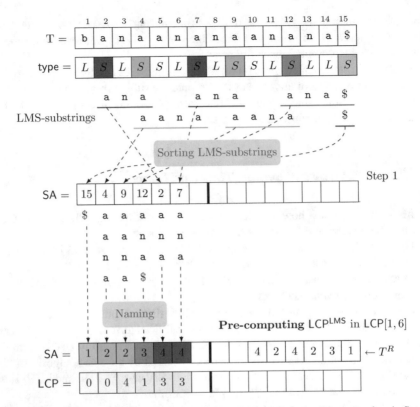

Fig. 4.5 Pre-computing LCP values between LMS-substrings during *naming* procedure in Step 1. For instance, the lcp between the LMS-substrings ana$ and ana is stored in LCP[5] = 3. Also, the reduced string $T^R = 424231$ is stored in SA[10, 15] (as discussed in Sect. 3.3.1.2)

$$\mathsf{PLCP^{LMS}}[\mathsf{SA}^R[i]] = \mathsf{LCP^{LMS}}[i], \text{ for } i = 1, \dots, n^R.$$

Then, the Φ-array (Definition 2.10) is computed by scanning SA^R as

$$\Phi[\mathsf{SA}^R[i]] = \mathsf{SA}^R[i-1], \text{ if } \mathsf{SA}^R[i] + 1 < n^R, \text{ for } i = 2, \dots, n^R.$$

The sparse Φ-algorithm must assess the distance between the LMS-suffixes being compared currently and their respective successors (in text order). $T[1, n]$ is scanned from right to left and these positions are stored in RA, in positions $\mathsf{SA}[n - n^R + 1, n]$, which are available at this point.

Then, $\mathsf{PLCP^{LMS}}$ is computed in linear time by Φ-algorithm into $\mathsf{LCP}[n - n^R + 1, n]$ considering Φ and RA arrays as

$$\mathsf{PLCP^{LMS}}[i] = \mathsf{lcp}(T_{\mathsf{RA}[i]}, T_{\mathsf{RA}[\Phi[i]]}), \text{ for } i = 1, \dots, n^R - 1.$$

The algorithm takes advantage of the precomputed values in $\mathsf{PLCP^{LMS}}[i]$ to start the computation of $\mathsf{lcp}(T_{\mathsf{RA}[i]}, T_{\mathsf{RA}[\varPhi[i]]})$, that is, suffixes $T_{\mathsf{RA}[i]}$ and $T_{\mathsf{RA}[\varPhi[i]]}$ are compared starting from at least their $\mathsf{PLCP^{LMS}}[i]$-th symbol.[1]

At the end, $\mathsf{LCP^{LMS}}$ is obtained from $\mathsf{PLCP^{LMS}}$, overwriting positions $\mathsf{LCP}[1, n^R]$ as

$$\mathsf{LCP^{LMS}}[i] = \mathsf{PLCP^{LMS}}[\mathsf{SA}^R[i]], \text{ for } i = 1, \dots, n^R.$$

Example Figure 4.6 illustrates Step 1 for $T = \text{banaanaaaaaaaa\$}$.

In Step 2, the LCP values in $\mathsf{LCP^{LMS}}$ are mapped into their corresponding positions in $\mathsf{LCP}[1, n]$ as in Sect. 4.2.1 (see Fig. 4.4).

In Steps 3 and 4, the second alternative to evaluate rmq (described in Sect. 4.2.1) can be improved in practice by using a stack as presented in Gog and Ohlebusch's paper [13]. The values in $C[c]$ are kept in sorted order, such that at each iteration, the minimum LCP value (rmq) is given by a binary search on $C[1, \sigma]$. The workspace with this alternative is added by the auxiliary data structures, which fit in 3σ words.

At the end, the LCP values between the last L-suffix and the first S-suffix of each c-bucket are computed by direct comparisons in overall linear time, as discussed previously.

Complexity Analysis
The running time of the resulting algorithm is $O(n\sigma)$ time, since the sparse $\varPhi$-algorithm used during Step 1 is linear [15] and the alternative chosen to solve rmq in Steps 3 and 4 (only at the top recursion level) runs in $O(\sigma)$ time for each induced suffix.

The workspace is reduced to 3σ words on top of what is needed to compute the suffix array, since $\mathsf{SA}[n - n^R + 1, n]$ and $\mathsf{LCP}[1, n]$ are reused through $\varPhi$-algorithm to compute $\mathsf{PLCP^{LMS}}$, which is used to obtain the final $\mathsf{LCP^{LMS}}$ in $\mathsf{LCP}[1, n^R]$. The additional space used to store $C[1, \sigma]$ is needed only during Steps 3 and 4, at the top recursion level, to solve rmq.

Louza et al. [18] implemented a variant of SACA-K, named SACA-K+LCP, that applies the above-mentioned procedures to compute the suffix array and the LCP array in $O(n\sigma)$ time using 4σ words of workspace.

---

[1] See Ohlebusch's book [27, Alg. 4.4] for details.

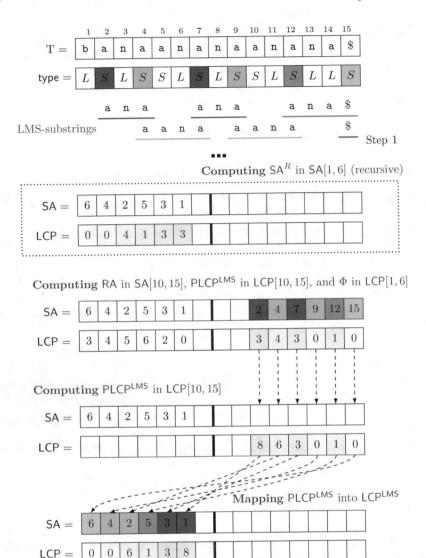

Fig. 4.6 Computing LCP^{LMS} at the end of Step 1. The LMS-suffixes are given sorted, such that SA^R is stored in SA[1, 6] and the precomputed LCP^{LMS} in LCP[1, 6]. First, the values in LCP^{LMS} are mapped into the partial PLCP^{LMS}, stored in LCP[10, 15]. For example, PLCP^{LMS}[1], stored in LCP[10], receives LCP^{LMS}[6] = 3, since SA^R[6] = 1. RA is computed in SA[10, 15], and Φ-array overwrites positions LCP[1, 6]. For example, RA[1], stored in SA[10], points to the text position $T[2]$, and RA[Φ[1]] = RA[3] = 7, which indicates that the first suffixes to be compared (in text order) by Φ-algorithm are T_2 and T_7. The precomputed value in PLCP[1], stored in LCP[10] = 3, indicates that PLCP[1] ≥ 3 and T_2 and T_7 can be compared starting from symbols $T[5]$ and $T[10]$. At the end, PLCP^{LMS} is computed in the same space LCP[10, 15], and the values are mapped into LCP[1, 6] to give the final LCP^{LMS}. PLCP^{LMS}[1] = 8 is mapped into LCP[6], since SA[6] = 1

Table 4.1 Running time (μs/input byte). Column 2 shows the alphabet size. Column 3 shows the collection size in MB

Dataset	σ	$n/2^{20}$	SA and LCP			SA	LCP
			SACA-K+LCP	SAIS+LCP [8]	SACA-K [24] and Φ [15]	SACA-K [24]	Φ-algorithm [15]
sources	230	201	0.26	**0.17**	0.24	0.21	0.03
xml	97	282	0.28	**0.18**	0.26	0.23	0.03
dna	16	385	0.38	**0.27**	0.36	0.31	0.05
english.1G	239	1,047	0.43	**0.31**	0.42	0.35	0.07
proteins	27	1,129	0.41	**0.30**	0.40	0.34	0.06
einstein-de	117	88	0.34	**0.18**	0.33	0.30	0.03
kernel	160	246	0.28	**0.16**	0.26	0.23	0.03
fib41	2	256	0.34	**0.18**	0.30	0.27	0.03
cere	5	440	0.34	**0.20**	0.31	0.28	0.03

The best results are shown in bold

4.3 Experiments

In this section we evaluate the performance of algorithmsSACA-K+LCP[2][18], SAIS+LCP[3][8], and SACA-K[4][24] followed by Φ-algorithm [15].

The algorithms were implemented in ANSI C, and their source codes are publicly available at https://github.com/felipelouza/sacak-lcp.

We used Pizza & Chili datasets.[5]In particular, datasets einstein-de, kernel, fib41, and cere are highly repetitive texts, and english.1G is the first 1GB of the original english dataset. We use 32-bits integers, and 1 byte for each symbol in $T[1, n]$.

The experiments were executed on a machine with Debian 7.0 GNU/Linux 64 bits operating system with an Intel processor i7-3770 at 3.4-GHz with 8 MB cache, 32 GB of RAM, and 2 TB of SATA storage. The sources were compiled using GNU GCC version 4.7.2, with the optimizing flag $-$O3 for all algorithms.

Running Time

Table 4.1 shows the running time of each algorithm in μsec/symbol. In all experiments, SAIS+LCP was the fastest algorithm. This result is similar to that

---

[2]https://github.com/felipelouza/sacak-lcp.

[3]https://github.com/kurpicz/sais-lite-lcp.

[4]code.google.com/archive/p/ge-nong/downloads.

[5]https://pizzachili.dcc.uchile.cl.

Table 4.2 Peakspace (bytes/input size). Column 2 shows the alphabet size. Column 3 shows the collection size in MB

			SA and LCP			SA	LCP
Dataset	σ	$n/2^{20}$	SACA-K+LCP	SAIS+LCP [8]	SACA-K [24] and Φ [15]	SACA-K [24]	Φ-algorithm [15]
sources	230	201	**9**	**9**	13	**5**	13
xml	97	282	**9**	**9**	13	**5**	13
dna	16	385	**9**	**9**	13	**5**	13
english.1G	239	1,047	**9**	**9**	13	**5**	13
proteins	27	1,129	**9**	**9**	13	**5**	13
einstein-de	117	88	**9**	**9**	13	**5**	13
kernel	160	246	**9**	**9**	13	**5**	13
fib41	2	256	**9**	**9**	13	**5**	13
cere	5	440	**9**	**9**	13	**5**	13

The best results are shown in bold

obtained by Nong [24, Table III], when comparing SACA-K with SAIS to compute only the suffix array. Note that, the relative difference between SACA-K+LCP and SAIS+LCP is "almost" constant.

We remark that SAIS+LCP is derived from the very optimized implementation of SAIS by Yuta Mori [10], named *sais-lite*.[6] When we compare SACA-K+LCP with SACA-K followed by Φ-algorithm we can see their similar speed, and we may conclude that the overhead added by computing the LCP array is small, while using less space as we show next.

Peakspace

Table 4.2 shows the peakspace of each algorithm, that is, the maximum memory used (at the same time), in bytes per symbol. SAIS+LCP and SACA-K+LCP presented the smallest values to compute SA and LCP, which is also similar to the results obtained by Nong [24, Table II], when comparing SACA-K with the implementation sais-lite.

We may conclude that, in practice, SAIS+LCP's peakspace is very close to the optimal space required by SACA-K+LCP. Φ-algorithm required $13n$ bytes since it has to simultaneously store T, SA and an additional array of n integers to compute the LCP array.

---

[6]https://sites.google.com/site/yuta256/.

Table 4.3 Workspace (bytes). Column 2 shows the alphabet size. Column 3 shows the collection size in MB

| Dataset | σ | $n/2^{20}$ | SA and LCP | | | SA | LCP |
			SACA-K+LCP	SAIS+LCP [8]	SACA-K [24] and Φ [15]	SACA-K [24]	Φ-algorithm [15]
sources	230	201	**10**	16	823,698	**1**	1,647,396
xml	97	282	**10**	14	1,156,781	**1**	2,313,562
dna	16	385	**10**	13	1,577,843	**1**	3,155,686
english.1G	239	1,047	**10**	15	4,287,904	**1**	8,575,808
proteins	27	1,129	**10**	13	4,625,201	**1**	9,250,402
einstein-de	117	88	**10**	14	362,338	**1**	724,676
kernel	160	246	**10**	14	1,007,662	**1**	2,015,324
fib41	2	256	**10**	13	1,046,540	**1**	2,093,080
cere	5	440	**10**	13	1,801,901	**1**	3,603,802

The best results are shown in bold

Workspace

Table 4.3 shows the workspace of each algorithm. The workspace was obtained by subtracting from the peakspace the space used by the input T ($1n$ bytes), and the output, that is, SA and LCP ($9n$ bytes) for columns 4–6, only SA ($4n$ bytes) for column 7, and only LCP ($4n$ bytes) for column 8.

SACA-K+LCP was the only algorithm that kept constant space usage across experiments to compute SA and LCP, namely 1 KB of SACA-K's workspace (as shown in column 7) added by 9 KB used by auxiliary data structures to solve rmq. Interestingly, SAIS+LCP also presented a small workspace, even though it has a worse theoretical bound. SACA-K's workspace was always 1 KB. The workspace of SACA-K combined with Φ-algorithm was much larger as it is dominated by the memory requirements of Φ-algorithm, which uses an additional array of n integers.

Conclusions

Overall, SAIS+LCP is the better alternative in practice to compute the suffix and LCP arrays. On the other hand, SACA-K+LCP is an improvement to the theoretical problem, achieving optimal time and space for constant alphabets, while preserving competitive practical performance of SACA-K.

References

1. A. Abeliuk, R. Cánovas, G. Navarro, Practical compressed suffix trees. Algorithms **6**(2), 319–351 (2013)
2. M.I. Abouelhoda, S. Kurtz, E. Ohlebusch, Replacing suffix trees with enhanced suffix arrays. J. Discrete Algorithms **2**(1), 53–86 (2004)
3. M.I. Abouelhoda, S. Kurtz, E. Ohlebusch, Enhanced suffix arrays and applications, in *Handbook on Computational Molecular Biology*, pp. 7–27 (Chapman and Hall/CRC, 2005)
4. T. Beller, S. Gog, E. Ohlebusch, T. Schnattinger, Computing the longest common prefix array based on the Burrows-Wheeler transform. J. Discrete Algorithms **18**, 22–31 (2013)
5. M. Burrows, D.J. Wheeler, A block-sorting lossless data compression algorithm. Technical report, Digital SRC Research Report, 1994
6. M. Cáceres, G. Navarro, Faster repetition-aware compressed suffix trees based on block trees, in *String Processing and Information Retrieval - 26th International Symposium, SPIRE 2019, Segovia, Spain, October 7–9, 2019, Proceedings*, pp. 434–451 (2019)
7. A. Farruggia, T. Gagie, G. Navarro, S.J. Puglisi, J. Sirén, Relative suffix trees. Comput. J. **61**(5), 773–788 (2018)
8. J. Fischer, Inducing the LCP-array, in *Proc. Workshop on Algorithms and Data Structures (WADS)*, pp. 374–385 (2011)
9. J. Fischer, V. Heun, A new succinct representation of rmq-information and improvements in the enhanced suffix array, in *Proc. Combinatorics, Algorithms, Probabilistic and Experimental Methodologies (ESCAPE)*, pp. 459–470 (2007)
10. J. Fischer, F. Kurpicz, Dismantling divsufsort, in *Proc. Prague Stringology Conference (PSC)*, pp. 62–76 (2017)
11. T. Gagie, G. Navarro, N. Prezza, Fully functional suffix trees and optimal text searching in BWT-runs bounded space. J. ACM **67**(1), 2:1–2:54 (2020)
12. S. Gog, *Compressed Suffix Trees: Design, Construction, and Applications*, Ph.D. thesis, University of Ulm, 2011
13. S. Gog, E. Ohlebusch, Fast and lightweight LCP-array construction algorithms, in *Proc. Workshop on Algorithm Engineering and Experimentation (ALENEX)*, pp. 25–34 (2011)
14. S. Gog, E. Ohlebusch, Compressed suffix trees: efficient computation and storage of LCP-values. J. Exp. Algorithmics (2013)
15. J. Kärkkäinen, G. Manzini, S.J. Puglisi, Permuted longest-common-prefix array, in *Proc. Annual Symposium on Combinatorial Pattern Matching (CPM)*, pp. 181–192 (2009)
16. T. Kasai, G. Lee, H. Arimura, S. Arikawa, K. Park, Linear-time longest-common-prefix computation in suffix arrays and its applications, in *Proc. Annual Symposium on Combinatorial Pattern Matching (CPM)*, pp. 181–192 (2001)
17. F.A. Louza, T. Gagie, G.P. Telles, Burrows-Wheeler transform and LCP array construction in constant space. J. Discrete Algorithms **42**, 14–22 (2017)
18. F.A. Louza, S. Gog, G.P. Telles, Optimal suffix sorting and LCP array construction for constant alphabets. Inf. Process. Lett. **118**, 30–34 (2017)
19. U. Manber, G. Myers, Suffix arrays: a new method for on-line string searches, in *Proc. ACM-SIAM Symposium on Discrete Algorithms (SODA)*, pp. 319–327 (1990)
20. G. Manzini, Two space saving tricks for linear time LCP array computation, in *Proc. Scandinavian Workshop on Algorithm Theory (SWAT)*, pp. 372–383 (2004)
21. G. Navarro, V. Mäkinen, Compressed full-text indexes. ACM Comput. Surv. **39**(1), 1–61 (2007)
22. G. Navarro, A.O. Pereira, Faster compressed suffix trees for repetitive collections. ACM J. Exp. Algorithmics **21**(1), 1.8:1–1.8:38 (2016)
23. G. Navarro, L.M.S. Russo, Fast fully-compressed suffix trees, in *Proc. IEEE Data Compression Conference (DCC)*, pp. 283–291 (2014)
24. G. Nong, Practical linear-time O(1)-workspace suffix sorting for constant alphabets. ACM Trans. Inf. Syst. **31**(3), 1–15 (2013)

25. G. Nong, S. Zhang, W.H. Chan, Two efficient algorithms for linear time suffix array construction. IEEE Trans. Comput. **60**(10), 1471–1484 (2011)
26. D.S.N. Nunes, M. Ayala-Rincón, A compressed suffix tree based implementation with low peak memory usage, in *Proc. XXXIX Latin American Computer Conference (CLEI)*, pp. 73–94 (2013)
27. E. Ohlebusch, *Bioinformatics Algorithms: Sequence Analysis, Genome Rearrangements and Phylogenetic Reconstruction* (Oldenbusch Verlag, 2013)
28. N. Prezza, G. Rosone, Space-efficient computation of the LCP array from the Burrows-Wheeler transform. CoRR (2019). abs/1901.05226
29. L.M.S. Russo, G. Navarro, A.L. Oliveira, Fully compressed suffix trees. ACM Trans. Algorithms **7**(4), 53:1–53:34 (2011)
30. K. Sadakane, Compressed suffix trees with full functionality. Theory Comput. Syst. **41**(4), 589–607 (2007)
31. P. Weiner, Linear pattern matching algorithms, in *Proc. Annual Symposium on Switching and Automata Theory (SWAT)*, pp. 1–11 (1973)

Chapter 5
Inducing the Document Array

5.1 Introduction

The document array [17] is a simple data structure commonly used together with the suffix array when indexing string collections. It determines to which document each suffix in the suffix array belongs. The document array can be represented in a compact form by using a bitvector [21, Section 7.7]. However, in applications where the document array is accessed sequentially (e.g. [1, 3, 8, 13, 22, 24]), it is important to have it stored explicitly [11].

The suffix array for a string collection can be computed using a standard suffix sorting algorithm over the concatenation of all strings. Although this approach is straightforward and have been used in different contexts and applications, it may deteriorate both the theoretical bounds and the practical behavior of many suffix sorting algorithms (see Sect. 2.2.4). Also, as observed by Egidi and Manzini [4], from the algorithmic point of view it makes no sense to ignore the fact that the input consists of distinct strings, and this additional information can be exploited to design faster algorithms.

In this chapter we show how to modify algorithms SAIS [20] and SACA-K [19] (described in Chap. 3) to compute the suffix array for a string collection. The algorithms, referred to as gSAIS and gSACA-K [12], receive as input the concatenation of all strings using the same symbol as separator, such that ties between equal suffixes from different strings are broken by the string ranks. This approach

---

This chapter is based on [12]. It was first published in: *Theor. Comput. Sci.* (v. 678) and republished here with the permission of the copyright holder.

	1	2	3	4	5	6	7	8	9	10	11	12	13	14	15	16	17	18	19
1. T^{cat} =	b	a	n	a	n	a	$\$_1$	a	n	a	b	a	$\$_2$	a	n	a	n	$\$_3$	#

	1	2	3	4	5	6	7	8	9	10	11	12	13	14	15	16	17	18	19
2. T^{cat} =	b	a	n	a	n	a	$\$$	a	n	a	b	a	$\$$	a	n	a	n	$\$$	#

Fig. 5.1 Concatenation alternatives for the collection T = {banana\$, anaba\$, anan\$}. Separator symbols are colored

is equivalent to using distinct symbols as separators, but without the drawback of increasing the alphabet size of the input.

In Sect. 5.2.2 we show how to extend algorithms gSAIS and gSACA-K to also compute the document array as a by-product of the suffix array construction. The algorithms, referred to as gSAIS+DA and gSACA-K+DA, maintain the same theoretical bounds of SAIS and SACA-K.

In Sect. 5.3 we present experiments that show that the practical performance of gSAIS and gSACA-K is better than their original versions applied to sort directly the concatenation of all strings. We also show the practical performance of the augmented algorithms gSAIS+DA and gSACA-K+DA that outperform the best known alternatives for computing the document array.

5.2 Suffix Sorting for String Collections

Given a collection of d strings $T = \{T^1, T^2, \ldots, T^d\}$ of lengths $n_1, n_2, \ldots, n_d$, the suffix array for T is computed for the concatenation of all strings into a single string $T^{cat}[1, N]$, where $N = (\Sigma_{i=1}^{d} n_i) + 1$.

There are two common approaches to concatenate all strings of T: (1) replacing the sentinel symbol \$ of T^i by a distinct symbol $\$_i$, with $\$_i < \$_j$ if and only if $i < j$; or (2) using the sentinel \$ as a separator symbol. In both cases, $T^{cat}[1, N]$ is terminated with a new sentinel symbol #, such that # is smaller than any other symbol.

Definition 5.1 The concatenating alternatives for T are

1. $T^{cat} = T^1[1, n_1 - 1] \cdot \$_1 \cdot T^2[1, n_2 - 1] \cdot \$_2 \cdots T^d[1, n_d - 1] \cdot \$_d \cdot \#$
2. $T^{cat} = T^1[1, n_1 - 1] \cdot \$ \ \cdot T^2[1, n_2 - 1] \cdot \$ \ \cdots T^d[1, n_d - 1] \cdot \$ \ \cdot \#$

Example Figure 5.1 shows an example of the concatenation alternatives for the string collection $T = \{banana\$, anaba\$, anan\$\}$.

Although both approaches are straightforward and have been used in different contexts and applications (e.g. [1, 5–10, 14, 18, 23, 24]), they have the following drawbacks. The first alternative increases the alphabet size of T^{cat} by the number of strings d, which may deteriorate the theoretical bounds of many algorithms, especially when millions of short strings are processed (e.g. DNA reads). Notice

Steps:

1. Sort the LMS-suffixes and store in an auxiliary array SA^R.

2. Scan SA^R from right to left, $i = n^R, n^R - 1, \ldots, 1$, and insert each corresponding LMS-suffix of T into the tail of its c-bucket in SA.

3. Scan SA from left to right, $i = 1, 2, \ldots, n$, and for each suffix $T_{SA[i]}$, if $T_{SA[i]-1}$ is an L-suffix, insert $SA[i] - 1$ into the head of its bucket.

4. Scan SA from right to left, $i = n, n - 1, \ldots, 1$, and for each suffix $T_{SA[i]}$, if $T_{SA[i]-1}$ is an S-suffix, insert $SA[i] - 1$ into the tail of its bucket.

Fig. 5.2 *IS algorithm*

that the workspace of SACA-K [19] increases to $\sigma + d + O(1)$ words, which is not optimal for a constant size input alphabet. On the other hand, the second alternative does not guarantee that equal suffixes of different strings T^i and T^j will be sorted with respect to i and j, in other words, ties will not be broken by the string rank, which may cause unnecessary comparisons during suffix sorting, depending on the order the strings are given in the collection.

There exists a generalization of the Burrows–Wheeler transform for string collections, called eBWT [15, 16], which is also computed through suffix sorting. However, it does not make use of sentinel symbols in strings of $\mathcal{T}$. The eBWT is computed efficiently [2] given the input collection in lexicographic order, that is, $T^1 < T^2 < \cdots < T^d$. We assume that the strings in $\mathcal{T}$ are not given in any particular order.

5.2.1 Inducing SA

In this section we show how to modify algorithms SAIS and SACA-K to compute the (generalized) suffix array for a string collection. The resulting algorithms will be referred to as gSAIS and gSACA-K [12].

We first recall the main steps of algorithms SAIS and SACA-K (shown again in Fig. 5.2. See also Sect. 3.3.1).

Also, recall that whenever a suffix position is inserted at the tail (or head) of a c-bucket in SA, the pointer bkt[c] is increased (or decreased) by one.

Example Figure 5.3 shows a running example of algorithm SAIS for T^{cat} created by concatenation alternative 2.

In what follows, we shall assume that the collection $\mathcal{T} = \{T^1, T^2, \ldots, T^d\}$ is concatenated into $T^{cat}[1, N] = T^1[1, n_1-1]\cdot\$\cdot T^2[1, n_2-1]\cdot\$ \cdots T^d[1, n_d-1]\cdot\$\cdot\#$ using the same symbol \$ as separator and a new sentinel symbol # (alternative 2). This alternative preserves the alphabet size.

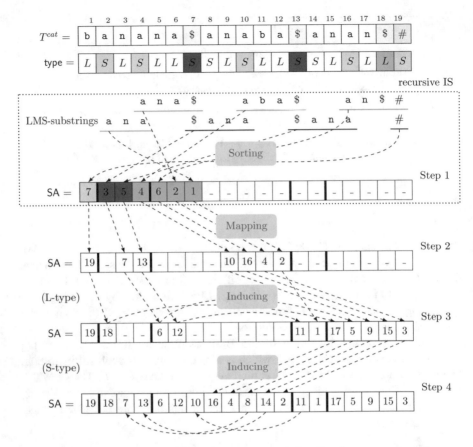

Fig. 5.3 Running example of algorithm *IS algorithm* applied to directly compute the suffix array for T^{cat} = banana\$anaba\$anan\$# created by alternative 2. The algorithm treats symbols \$ as any other symbol of the alphabet. Note that for T^{cat} created by alternative 1 the final entries in SA[2, 4] would be [7, 13, 18], given $\$_1 < \$_2 < \#_3$. Step 1 is executed recursively, but it is not an issue here; as we will see, modifications on SAIS and SACA-K are necessary only at the top recursion level in order to adapt them to compute the suffix array for string collections. Colors are used to help visually mapping suffixes through the algorithm. Colors will have the same meaning in the following figures as well

We consider an augmented relative order among separator symbols \$ in $T^{cat}[1, N]$, such that a \$ from string T^i will be smaller than a \$ from string T^j if and only if $i < j$, that is, a separator in $T^{cat}[i'] = \$$ will be smaller than $T^{cat}[j'] = \$$ if and only if $i' < j'$. The algorithms will implicitly use this relative order to produce the same suffix ordering that would be generated by using different separators, one for each string T^i in $\mathcal{T}$.

The key observation to modify SAIS and SACA-K is that every suffix in T^{cat} starting with a symbol \$ is an LMS-suffix, except for the last one, namely $T^{cat}_{N-1} =$

\$#, which is an L-suffix, since by definition # < \$. We will see that these suffixes can be sorted separately in an additional linear scan over T^{cat}.

Example Figure 5.3 also shows the suffix classification for the string $T^{cat} =$ banana\$anaba\$anan\$#. The LMS-substrings starting with \$ are highlighted.

Recall that within each c-bucket of SA, L-suffixes are smaller than S-suffixes. This is not the case for the \$-bucket, where the L-suffix $T^{cat}_{N-1} = \$\#$ should be the largest suffix. To guarantee that, the \$-bucket is handled as a special case during Steps 1 and 2.

In Step 1, when the LMS-substrings of T^{cat} are sorted using a modified version of *IS algorithm*, we reserve the last position of the \$-bucket to T^{cat}_{N-1}, that is, the LMS-suffixes starting with \$ are bucket sorted in Step 2' starting from position bkt[\$] − 1, where bkt[\$] is the tail of \$-bucket. Then, at the end of Step 2', we insert the suffix T^{cat}_{N-1} directly at that reserved position of \$-bucket. Steps 3' and 4' work exactly the same.

Another important observation, from a practical standpoint, is that the LMS-suffixes starting with \$ generate LMS-substrings that will be sorted unnecessarily, since both SAIS and SACA-K treat symbols \$ as any other symbol, but if two suffixes are equal up to the first occurrence of \$, then their symbols should not be compared any further.

Then, the LMS-substring sorting procedure may be speed up. To do that, when $T^{cat}[1, N]$ is scanned from right to left to bucket sort all LMS-suffixes, we do not insert any LMS-suffix T^{cat}_j in its corresponding c-bucket if the next LMS-suffix T^{cat}_i (to the left) starts with symbol \$, for $1 < i < j \leq n$. The intuition is that these positions j are exactly those that will induce the order of the LMS-substrings starting at positions i, which are unnecessary. In practice, as the scan is performed from right to left, T^{cat}_j is inserted into its bucket, but whenever T^{cat}_i starts with \$, T^{cat}_j is removed.

Therefore, after sorting all LMS-substrings (except those starting with \$), we scan $T^{cat}[1, N]$ again, this time from left to right, and the LMS-suffixes starting with \$ are inserted directly into the \$-bucket (in order), starting from the head of the \$-bucket. At the end, the LMS-substrings are mapped into the beginning of SA, and the LMS-substrings starting with \$ are sorted correctly, according to their positions in T^{cat}.

Example Figure 5.4 shows Step 1 adapted to sort the LMS-substrings of $T^{cat} =$ banana\$anaba\$anan\$.

Then, *naming* takes place considering the augmented order among \$ symbols in T^{cat}, such that each LMS-substring starting with \$ will receive a different name according to its position in SA. To do that, SA[1, N] is scanned from left to right and consecutive LMS-substrings are compared. When LMS-substrings start with \$, we do not have to compare the substrings, but just assign increasing names according to their positions in SA. In other words, given two LMS-substrings starting with \$, say s_i and s_j with names r_i and r_j, we have $r_i < r_j$ if and only if $i < j$. Also,

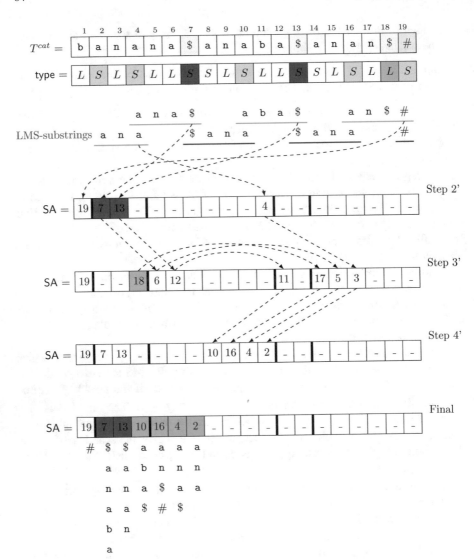

Fig. 5.4 Sorting all LMS-substrings with modified *IS algorithm* considering the augmented relative order among separator symbols. In Step 2' bucket sorting does not insert the positions 16 and 10 of T^{cat} into their c-buckets, since they follow an LMS-suffix starting with $, which would induce the order of the LMS-substrings $T^{cat}[13, 16]$ and $T^{cat}[7, 10]$. The order of these substrings is set in SA after sorting all LMS-substrings in Step 4'. Also, notice that the last position in the $-bucket is reserved to the L-suffix T_{18}^{cat} during the bucket sorting in Step 2'. T_{18}^{cat} will be inserted directly in SA[4] in Step 2 (see Fig. 5.6). At the end, all LMS-substrings are sorted accordingly

when two consecutive LMS-substrings $T^{cat}[i, j]$ and $T^{cat}[i', j']$ are equal up to $, $T^{cat}[i, j] < T^{cat}[i', j']$ if and only if $i < i'$, which may speed up the naming procedure in practice.

The reduced string T^R is created as usual, according to SAIS and SACA-K approaches.

Example Figure 5.5 shows the modified *naming* procedure, where LMS-substrings starting with $ are not explicitly compared, their names are given according to their positions in SA. The figure also shows the resulting reduced string T^R created after sorting all LMS-substrings.

Fortunately, the above modifications in Step 1 are necessary only at the top recursion level of both SAIS and SACA-K, since the reduced string T^R will be exactly the same as the one produced by the original algorithms when applied to sort the suffixes of T^{cat} created using concatenation alternative 1. The recursive call to sort all LMS-suffixes is done using the original algorithms.

In Step 2, the last position of the $-bucket is reserved for the L-suffix T^{cat}_{N-1}, which is inserted at the end of Step 2.

In Steps 3 and 4, we do not induce any L- or S-suffix $T^{cat}_{SA[i]-1}$ starting with $. Therefore, we preserve the relative order of suffixes that are equal up to $.

Then, at the end of Step 4, we perform a sequential scan over $T^{cat}[1, N]$ and the suffixes starting with $ are positioned in the $-bucket so that the augmented order is respected.

Example Figure 5.6 shows a running example with the adapted algorithm to sort all suffixes of $T^{cat} = $ banana\$anaba\$anan\$#. In Step 2, the position SA[4] is reserved for suffix T^{cat}_{18}. Note that no suffix starting with a $ symbol is induced during Steps 3 and 4. At the end, suffixes T^{cat}_7, T^{cat}_{13}, T^{cat}_{18} are inserted in the $-bucket in the correct order.

Complexity Analysis

The running time of the modified versions, referred to as gSAIS and gSACA-K [12], remains $O(N)$, since we only added two sequential scan over T^{cat} at the recursion top level to directly bucket sort suffixes starting with $. Moreover, we avoid sorting exactly $d - 1$ LMS-substrings in Step 1, which may improve the practical performance of the algorithms, as shown in the experiments (Sect. 5.3).

The workspace of gSAIS and gSACA-K has the same of their original versions when applied to sort T^{cat} created by alternative 2, that is, N bits plus $O(\sigma)$ words and $\sigma + O(1)$ words. However, recall that alternative 2 does not guarantee the relative order among suffixes that are equal up to $.

A theoretical improvement is achieved when comparing gSACA-K with the original SACA-K applied to sort T^{cat} created by alternative 1. In particular, the workspace of SACA-K is $\sigma + d + O(1)$ words, whereas the workspace of gSACA-K remains $\sigma + O(1)$ words, which is optimal for constant alphabets. We will see the effect of such differences in practice in the experiments (Sect. 5.3).

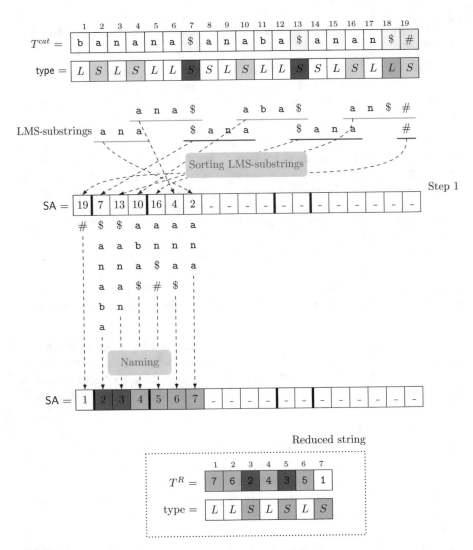

Fig. 5.5 Step 1, *naming* procedure, modified to consider $ symbols as different symbols. For instance, LMS-substrings $T^{cat}[7, 10]$ and $T^{cat}[13, 17]$ are not compared symbol by symbol, their names (ranks) are given according to their positions in SA. At the end, the reduced string $T^R = 7624351$ is created. Note that all LMS-substrings starting with $ have different ranks

5.2.2 Inducing SA and DA

In this section we show how to modify gSAIS and gSACA-K to also compute the document array during the suffix array construction.

The key observation to compute DA during gSAIS and gSACA-K is that given DA values of all LMS-suffixes (only at the top recursive level), we can induce the document array during Steps 3 and 4. Moreover, DA values of all LMS-suffixes can be computed with $O(1)$ additional cost during Step 2 as follows.

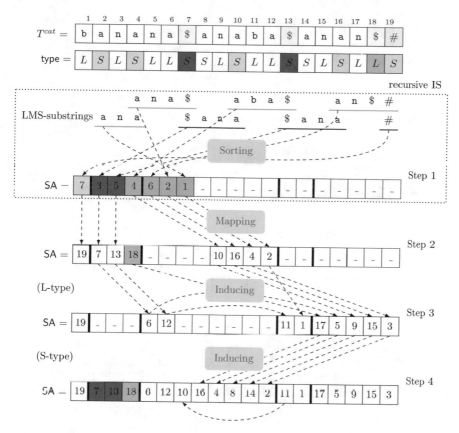

Fig. 5.6 Running example of modified *IS algorithm* to compute the suffix array for $T^{cat} = banana\$anaba\$anan\$\#$

In Step 2, the suffix array SA^R of the reduced string is given in the first half of SA, that is, $\mathsf{SA}[1, n/2 - 1]$. Then, ISA^R is computed and stored in $\mathsf{SA}[n/2, n]$ as follows. For $i = 1, \ldots, n^R$, $\mathsf{ISA}^R[\mathsf{SA}^R[i]] = i$. In the sequel, $T^{cat}[1, N]$ is scanned from right to left to map suffixes from T^R to the LMS-suffixes of T^{cat}. We take advantage of this scanning to compute the DA values of all LMS-suffixes in constant time. Starting from $i = N, N-1, \ldots, 1$, $j = n^R$ and $k = d+1$, whenever $T^{cat}[i] = \$$, k is decremented by one. When T_i^{cat} is an LMS-suffix, $\mathsf{SA}^R[\mathsf{ISA}^R[j]] = i$, j is decremented by one, and the value in $\mathsf{DA}[\mathsf{ISA}^R[j]]$ receives k, which corresponds to the index of the string which T_i^{cat} came from.

At the end of Step 2, when T_{N-1}^{cat} is inserted directly at the tail of \$-bucket, we also set the value of such position in DA as d, since we know that suffix T_{N-1}^{cat} came from T^d.

Example Figure 5.7 shows Step 2 modified to compute DA values for all LMS-suffixes in SA.

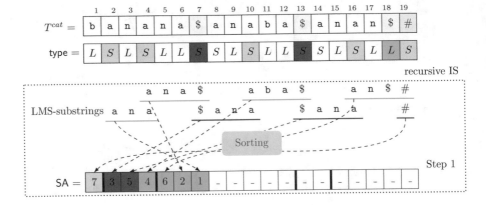

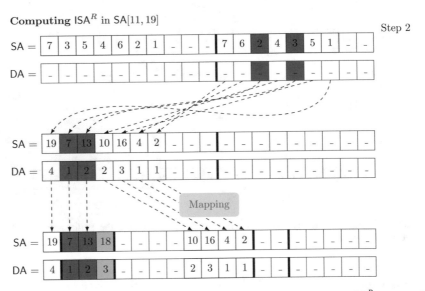

Fig. 5.7 Computing DA in Step 2 for $T^{cat} = banana\$anaba\$anan\$\#$. Initially, SA^R, computed in Step 1, is used to compute ISA^R, which are stored in SA[1, 7] and SA[11, 17], respectively. Then $T^{cat}[1, 19]$ is scanned from right to left and the values $\{1, 5, 3, 4, 2, 6, 7\}$ are mapped to $\{19, 16, 13, 10, 7, 4, 2\}$, that is, the suffix in $SA^R[1]$ corresponds to the LMS-suffix T_{19}^{cat}, the suffix in $SA^R[5]$ corresponds to T_{16}^{cat}, and so on. When the scan finds the third \$ in $T^{cat}[7]$, k is equal to $d + 1 - 3 = 1$, and the values in DA[2], DA[6], and DA[7] are equal to 1, that is, the suffixes in these positions in SA^R came from string T^1. At the end, the values in SA^R and DA are mapped into their corresponding buckets in SA and DA starting from the tail of each bucket. Recall that the last position of \$-bucket is reserved to T_{N-1}^{cat}, which is inserted directly at the end of Step 2 together with its value in DA, that is, SA[4] = 18 and DA[4] = 3

In Step 3, whenever $SA[i] = j$ induces T_{j-1}^{cat} (L-suffix) in position $SA[k]$, the value in DA[k] is induced by DA[i], which is already computed in DA, since T_j^{cat} is either an LMS-suffix or it is an L-suffix that has been induced in Step 3.

Step 4 is symmetric to Step 3.

At the end of Step 4, when $T^{cat}[1, N]$ is scanned to bucket sort all suffixes starting with $, we also compute the DA values of these suffixes, considering their positions in T^{cat}.

The correctness of the algorithm comes from the fact that the DA values of the LMS-suffixes, computed in Step 2, induce all values in DA (first the L-suffixes in Step 3, then the S-suffixes in Step 4), and since we do not induce L- or S-suffixes starting with $ in Steps 3 and 4, once a suffix is induced in position SA[k], the value in DA[k] does not change. Therefore, DA is filled entirely with the correct values.

Example Figure 5.8 shows a running example with the modified algorithm to compute the suffix array and the document array for T^{cat} = banana$anaba$anan$#.

Complexity Analysis
The modified algorithms, referred to as gSAIS+DA and gSACA-K+DA, maintain the theoretical bounds of their original versions, that is, $O(N)$ time, since we added only a constant cost operation in Step 2 to obtain each DA value, which are moved together with the values in SA during Steps 3 and 4. The DA values of suffixes starting with $ are given directly when they are positioned at the end of Step 4.

The workspace of gSAIS+DA and gSACA-K+DA remains the same as their original algorithms, namely N bits plus $O(\sigma)$ words and $\sigma + O(1)$ words, respectively. Therefore, gSACA-K+DA's workspace is optimal for strings from constant alphabets.

5.3 Experiments

In this section we evaluate the performance of algorithms gSAIS, gSACA-K, gSAIS+DA, gSACA-K+DA [12] with their original version SAIS [20] and SACA-K [19]. The algorithms were implemented in ANSI C based on the source codes of SAIS[1] and SACA-K.[2]

The source code of all algorithms and detailed experimental results are publicly available at github.com/felipelouza/gsa-is.

The experiments were conducted on a machine with `Debian GNU/Linux 8` (kernel 3.16.0-4) 64 bits operating system with an `Intel Xeon` processor `E5-2630 v3` 2.40-GHz with 20 MB of cache, 386 GB of RAM and a 13 TB SATA storage. The sources were compiled using GNU GCC version 4.9.2, with optimizing flag $-$O3.

The time was measured using the `clock()` function of C and the workspace was obtained by subtracting the memory used by input and by output from the total peak

---

[1] https://sites.google.com/site/yuta256/.

[2] code.google.com/archive/p/ge-nong/downloads.

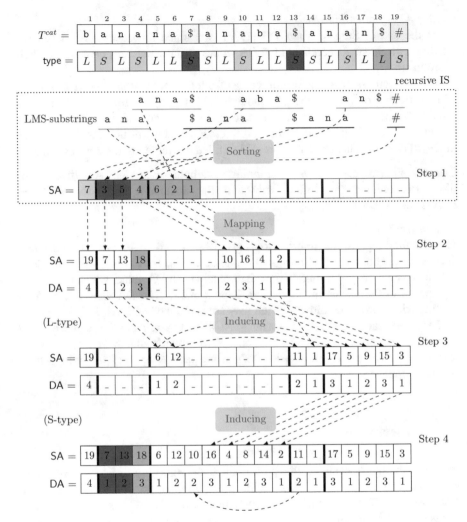

Fig. 5.8 Running example for $T^{cat} = banana\$anaba\$anan\$\#$. Suffixes T_7^{cat}, T_{13}^{cat}, and T_{18}^{cat}, starting with \$, are inserted sequentially at the end of Step 4, with the corresponding DA values inserted in order

memory measured by `malloc_count` library.[3] We used 32-bits integers when $N < 2^{31}$, otherwise we used 64-bits integers. Each symbol of T^{cat} uses 1 byte, unless otherwise stated.

We used real datasets of size up to 16 GB with strings from different application domains, described in Table 5.1. The experiments took about 10 days of computing to finish.

---

[3]panthema.net/2013/malloc_count.

Table 5.1 Datasets. Column 2 shows the alphabet size. Column 3 shows the collection size in GB. Column 4 shows the number of strings. Column 5 and 6 show the average and maximum length of the strings. Columns 7 and 8 show the average and maximum lcp values computed on the single strings, which provide an approximation for suffix sorting difficulty

Dataset	σ	$N/2^{30}$	d	N/d	$max(n_i)$	$mean\_lcp$	max_lcp
pages	205	3.74	1,000	4,019,585	362,724,758	29,595.13	2,912,604
revision	203	0.39	20,433	20,527	2,000,452	31,612.79	1,995,055
influenza	15	0.56	394,217	1,516	2,867	533.83	2,379
wikipedia	208	8.32	3,903,703	2,288	224,488	27.12	61,055
reads	4	2.87	32,621,862	94	101	43.35	101
proteins	25	15.77	50,825,784	333	36,805	91.03	32,882

Description:

- pages is a repetitive collection from a snapshot of the Finnish-language edition of Wikipedia. Each document is composed by one page and its revisions[4]
- revision is the same as pages, except that each revision is a separate document
- influenza is a repetitive collection of the genomes of influenza viruses[5]
- wikipedia is a collection of pages from a snapshot of the English-language edition of Wikipedia[6]
- reads is a collection of DNA sequencing reads from Human Chromosome 14 (library 1)[7]
- proteins is a collection of protein sequences from Uniprot/TrEMBL protein database release 2015_09[8]

5.3.1 Computing SA

We compared the performance of gSAIS and gSACA-K with the original algorithms SAIS and SACA-K applied to sort T^{cat} created by alternatives 1 and 2 (see Definition 5.1). SAIS and SACA-K will be referred to as SAIS* and SACA-K* when sorting T^{cat} created by alternative 1, otherwise they will be referred to as SAIS and SACA-K. SAIS* and SACA-K* use an array of integers to store the concatenated string T^{cat}, which occupies $4N$ bytes when $N < 2^{31}$ and $8N$ bytes otherwise.

Recall that the suffix array produced by algorithms gSAIS and gSACA-K is the same as the one produced by SAIS* and SACA-K*, whereas the output of SAIS and SACA-K can be slightly different, since they do not guarantee the relative order among suffixes that are equal up to the separator (see Fig. 5.3).

---

[4] jltsiren.kapsi.fi/data/fiwiki.bz2.

[5] ftp.ncbi.nih.gov/genomes/INFLUENZA/influenza.fna.gz.

[6] algo2.iti.kit.edu/gog/projects/ALENEX15/collections/ENWIKIBIG/.

[7] gage.cbcb.umd.edu/data/index.html.

[8] www.ebi.ac.uk/uniprot/download-center/.

Running Time

Figure 5.9 shows the running time of each algorithm in μsec/symbol. gSACA-K and SACA-K were the fastest. In particular, gSACA-K was faster than SACA-K when the number of strings d is large, as in `proteins` (up to 7.7%) and `reads` (up to 10.6%), since it avoids sorting $(d - 1)$ LMS-substrings at the top recursion level. Comparing gSACA-K with SACA-K*, which produces the same output, the time spent by gSACA-K was 24.3% smaller on the average. SACA-K* was the slowest algorithm due to cache effects caused by the larger integer array used to store $T^{cat}[1, N]$. We can see that the relative difference between gSAIS and gSACA-K is almost constant, similarly to the results obtained by Nong [19, Table III] when comparing SAIS with SACA-K.

Peakspace

Figure 5.10 shows the peak memory usage of each algorithm in bytes per symbol. Observe that when the total size $N \geq 2^{31}$, the peak memory of all algorithms increases, since they use 64-bits integers.

SACA-K and gSACA-K presented the smallest values, which correspond to their theoretical space of $5N+O(1)$ bytes when $N < 2^{31}$ and $9N+O(1)$ bytes otherwise. SAIS* and SACA-K* used more memory, since the concatenated string T^{cat} is stored in an array of integers whose size doubles when $N \geq 2^{31}$. Moreover, the augmented alphabet of size $\sigma + d$ also increases the space used by the bucket array bkt of SAIS* and SACA-K*, especially for datasets with many strings.

Workspace

Figure 5.11 shows the workspace of each algorithm in MB. The workspace was obtained by subtracting the space used by T^{cat} and SA from the peakspace. SAIS* and SACA-K* use $8N$ bytes for T^{cat} and SA when $N < 2^{31}$, otherwise they use $16N$ bytes. SAIS, SACA-K, gSAIS, and gSACA-K use $5N$ bytes for T^{cat} and SA when $N < 2^{31}$, otherwise they use $9N$ bytes.

SACA-K and gSACA-K presented the smallest values, which are optimal for constant alphabets, corresponding to 1 KB when $N < 2^{31}$ and 2 KB otherwise. The workspace of SAIS*, SAIS, and gSAIS are linearly dependent on the length of T^{cat}, whereas the workspace of SACA-K* is linearly dependent on the number of strings.

Conclusions

Overall, gSACA-K's time-space trade-off is Pareto optimal compared to all the other algorithms in the experiments. Moreover, gSACA-K (and gSAIS) outputs a suffix array where the relative order among suffixes that are equal up to the separator is respected.

5.3.2 Computing SA and DA

We compared the performance of gSAIS+DA and gSACA-K+DA with algorithms gSAIS and gSACA-K combined with the linear algorithm that computes DA[1, N]

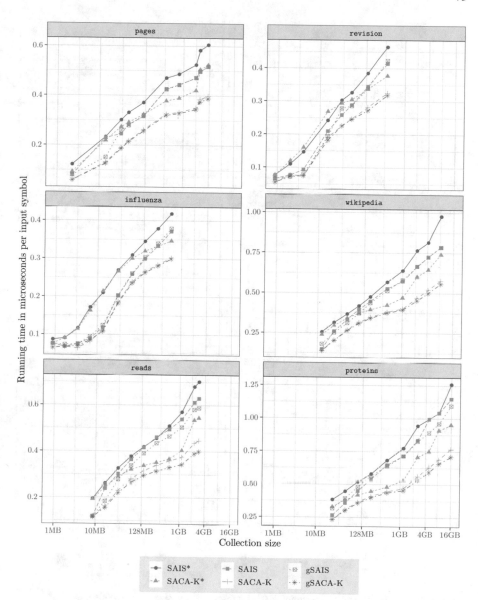

Fig. 5.9 Running time to compute SA with respect to the size of each collection

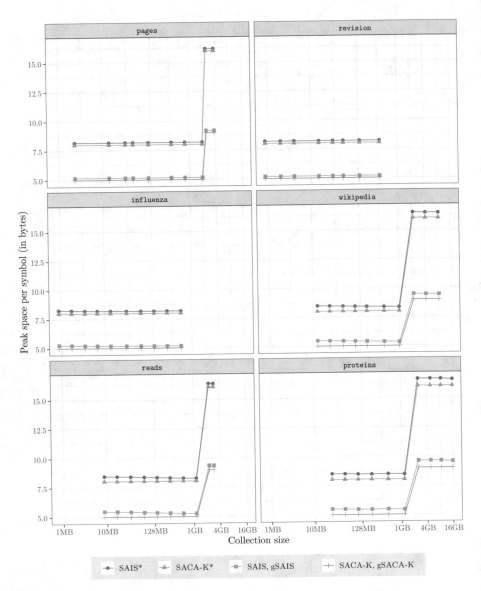

Fig. 5.10 Peakspace usage to compute SA with respect to the size of each collection

from its compact representation [21, Alg. 7.29] (see Sect. 2.2.4). We evaluated two versions, using uncompressed bitvectors, referred to as BIT, and using compressed bitvectors, referred to as BIT_SD, given by the SDSL library [7] version 2.0. The codes for BIT and BIT_SD were implemented in C++ and compiled by GNU G++ version 4.9.2, with optimizing flag −O3.

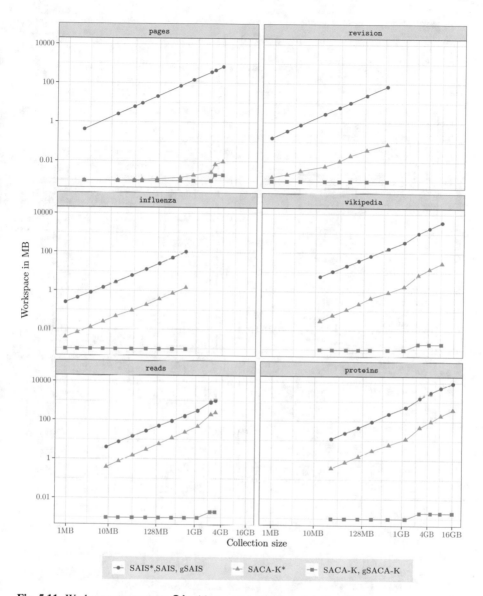

Fig. 5.11 Workspace to compute SA with respect to the size of each collection

Running Time

Figure 5.12 shows the running time of each algorithm in μsec/symbol. gSACA-K+DA and gSACA-K combined with BIT were the fastest alternatives. Comparing this figure to Fig. 5.9, we can see that the overhead added by computing the document array in gSACA-K+DA was small, 8.3% on the average. The time added by BIT was 10.2% in gSACA-K and BIT, on the average. Note that BIT was about 62.5% faster than BIT_SD.

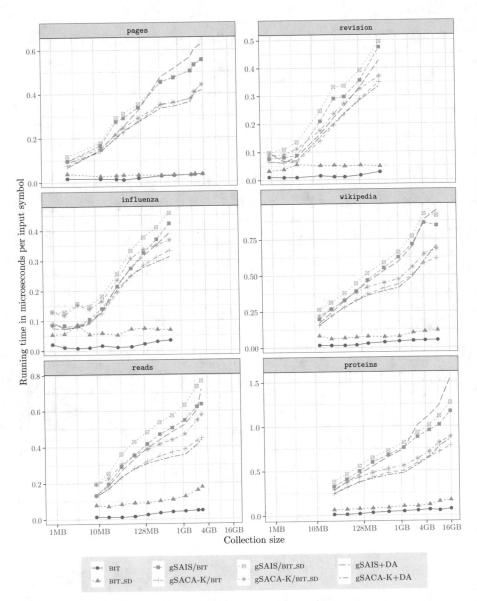

Fig. 5.12 Running time to compute SA and DA with respect to the size of each collection

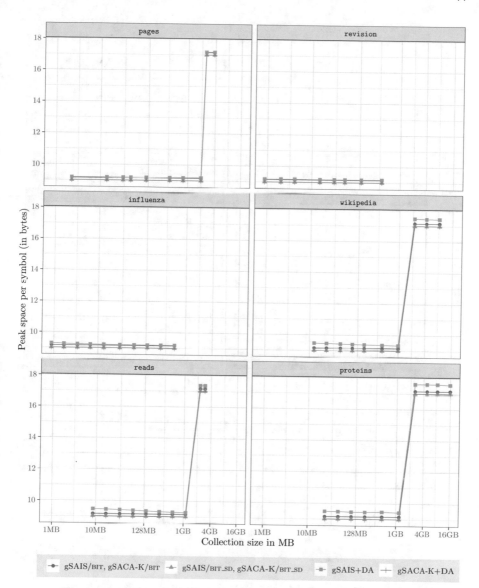

Fig. 5.13 Peakspace usage to compute SA and DA with respect to the size of each collection

Peakspace

Figure 5.13 shows the peak memory usage of each algorithm in bytes per symbol. gSACA-K+DA presented the smallest values, corresponding to its theoretical space of $9N + O(1)$ bytes when $N < 2^{31}$ and $17N + O(1)$ bytes, otherwise.

The peak memory of gSAIS and BIT_SD and gSACA-K and BIT_SD was similar to the values of gSACA-K+DA, only 0.03% larger on the average, which corre-

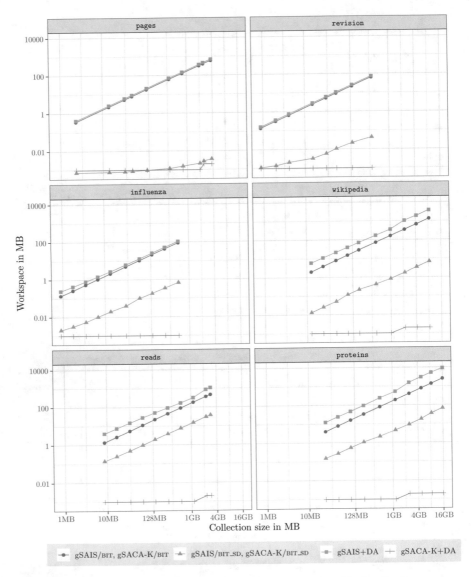

Fig. 5.14 Workspace to compute SA and DA with respect to the size of each collection

sponds to the $o(n)$ bits required by BIT_SD to solve rank queries. Also, note that the peak memory usage of BIT_SD was about 1.53% smaller than the space of BIT.

Workspace
Figure 5.14 shows the workspace of each algorithm in MB. The workspace was obtained by subtracting the space used by T^{cat}, SA, and DA from the peakspace.

All algorithms use $9N$ bytes for T^{cat}, SA and DA when $N < 2^{31}$, otherwise they use $17N$ bytes.

gSACA-K+DA presented the smallest values, which is optimal for constant alphabets, having 1 KB when $N < 2^{31}$ and 2 KB otherwise. The workspace of gSAIS+DA is larger than gSAIS and BIT because in gSAIS and BIT we first execute gSAIS and then BIT (the same for gSAIS and BIT_SD). The workspace of gSAIS+DA is linearly dependent on the length of N (inherited from gSAIS). The combined algorithms are dominated by the workspace of BIT and BIT_SD, which use $N + o(n)$ bits and $2d + \log \frac{N}{d} + o(d)$ bits to store B[1, N], respectively, for the rank enabled bitvector in addition to the space of T^{cat}, SA, and DA.

Conclusions

Overall, gSACA-K+DA's time-space trade-off is also Pareto optimal compared to all other solutions to compute SA and DA given T^{cat}.

References

1. M. Arnold, E. Ohlebusch, Linear time algorithms for generalizations of the longest common substring problem. Algorithmica **60**(4), 806–818 (2011)
2. S. Bonomo, S. Mantaci, A. Restivo, G. Rosone, M. Sciortino, Sorting conjugates and suffixes of words in a multiset. Int. J. Found. Comput. Sci. **25**(8), 1161 (2014)
3. L. Egidi, F.A. Louza, G. Manzini, G.P. Telles, External memory BWT and LCP computation for sequence collections with applications. Algorithms Mol. Biol. **14**(1), 6:1–6:15 (2019)
4. L. Egidi, G. Manzini, Lightweight BWT and LCP merging via the gap algorithm, in *Proc. International Symposium on String Processing and Information Retrieval (SPIRE)*, pp. 176–190 (2017)
5. T. Gagie, A. Hartikainen, J. Kärkkäinen, G. Navarro, S.J. Puglisi, J. Sirén, Document counting in compressed space, in *Proc. IEEE Data Compression Conference (DCC)*, pp. 103–112 (2015)
6. T. Gagie, K. Karhu, G. Navarro, S.J. Puglisi, J. Sirén, Document listing on repetitive collections, in *Proc. Annual Symposium on Combinatorial Pattern Matching (CPM)*, pp. 107–119 (2013)
7. S. Gog, T. Beller, A. Moffat, M. Petri, From theory to practice: plug and play with succinct data structures, in *Proc. Symposium on Experimental and Efficient Algorithms (SEA)*, vol. 8504 of *LNCS*, pp. 326–337 (Springer, 2014)
8. V. Guerrini, G. Rosone, Lightweight metagenomic classification via eBWT, in *Proc. International Conference on Algorithms for Computational Biology (AICoB)*, pp. 112–124 (2019)
9. T. Kopelowitz, G. Kucherov, Y. Nekrich, T. Starikovskaya, Cross-document pattern matching. J. Discrete Algorithms **24**, 40–47 (2014)
10. H. Li, Fast construction of FM-index for long sequence reads. Bioinformatics **30**(22), 3274–3275 (2014)
11. F.A. Louza, A simple algorithm for computing the document array. Inf. Process. Lett. **154** (2020)
12. F.A. Louza, S. Gog, G.P. Telles, Inducing enhanced suffix arrays for string collections. Theor. Comput. Sci. **678**, 22–39 (2017)
13. F.A. Louza, G.P. Telles, S. Gog, L. Zhao, Algorithms to compute the Burrows-Wheeler similarity distribution. Theor. Comput. Sci. **782**, 145–156 (2019)

14. V. Mäkinen, G. Navarro, J. Sirén, N. Välimäki, Storage and retrieval of highly repetitive sequence collections. J. Comput. Biol. **17**(3), 281–308 (2010)
15. S. Mantaci, A. Restivo, G. Rosone, M. Sciortino, An extension of the Burrows-Wheeler transform. Theor. Comput. Sci. **387**(3), 298–312 (2007)
16. S. Mantaci, A. Restivo, G. Rosone, M. Sciortino, A new combinatorial approach to sequence comparison. Theory Comput. Syst. **42**(3), 411–429 (2008)
17. S. Muthukrishnan, Efficient algorithms for document retrieval problems, in *Proc. ACM-SIAM Symposium on Discrete Algorithms (SODA)*, pp. 657–666 (2002)
18. G. Navarro, S.V. Thankachan, New space/time tradeoffs for top-k document retrieval on sequences. Theor. Comput. Sci. **542**, 83–97 (2014)
19. G. Nong, Practical linear-time O(1)-workspace suffix sorting for constant alphabets. ACM Trans. Inf. Syst. **31**(3), 1–15 (2013)
20. G. Nong, S. Zhang, W.H. Chan, Two efficient algorithms for linear time suffix array construction. IEEE Trans. Comput. **60**(10), 1471–1484 (2011)
21. E. Ohlebusch, *Bioinformatics Algorithms: Sequence Analysis, Genome Rearrangements and Phylogenetic Reconstruction* (Oldenbusch Verlag, 2013)
22. E. Ohlebusch, S. Gog, Efficient algorithms for the all-pairs suffix-prefix problem and the all-pairs substring-prefix problem. Inf. Process. Lett. **110**(3), 123–128 (2010)
23. J.T. Simpson, R. Durbin, Efficient construction of an assembly string graph using the FM-index. Bioinformatics **26**(12), i367–i373 (2010)
24. W.H.A. Tustumi, S. Gog, G.P. Telles, F.A. Louza, An improved algorithm for the all-pairs suffix-prefix problem. J. Discrete Algorithms **37**, 34–43 (2016)

Chapter 6
Inducing the Lyndon Array

6.1 Introduction

The Lyndon array is a powerful data structure that generalizes the idea of Lyndon factorization [6]. Lyndon arrays are equivalent to the Lyndon trees, introduced by Hohlweg and Reutenauer [11]. Interest in Lyndon arrays has been sparked since Bannai et al. [2] used them to prove a long-standing conjectured by Kolpakov and Kucherov [13] that the number of runs (maximal periodicities) in a string of length n is smaller than n.

Several algorithms to compute Lyndon arrays have been proposed in the past years (see [6–8]). Most of them compute the suffix array [19] as a preliminary data structure to compute the Lyndon array in linear time. Franek et al. [9] show that there exists a linear co-equivalence between the computation of Lyndon arrays and the suffix sorting. In fact, it has been observed by C. Diegelmann that Baier's suffix array construction algorithm [1] computes a permuted version of the Lyndon array in its first phase [8]. The Lyndon array can also be derived in linear time from the Lyndon tree [4], or alternatively, it can be obtained during the Burrows–Wheeler inversion [17].

The suffix array is a central data structure for string processing (see [18, 20, 24]). Suffix array construction has been extensively studied in the literature [12, 26] (see Chap. 3). Since the introduction of the algorithms SAIS [22] and SACA-K [21] that compute suffix arrays in linear time and are fast in practice, many solutions

This chapter is based on [16]. It was first published in: *Lecture Notes in Computer Science* (v. 11811) and republished here with the permission of the copyright holder.

adapting them have been proposed to the computation of related data structures, such as the Burrows–Wheeler transform [3, 25], the LCP array [5, 15] (see Chap. 4), the document array [14] (see Chap. 5), and others (e.g. [10, 23]).

In this chapter we present a variant of algorithm SACA-K [21], introduced in [16], that computes the Lyndon array in linear time during the suffix array construction. The algorithm uses $\sigma + O(1)$ words of workspace, which is optimal for strings from constant alphabets. In Sect. 6.3 we show experiments that compare this augmented suffix sorting algorithm with other linear time alternatives that compute Lyndon arrays.

6.2 Inducing the Lyndon Array

In this section we show how to modify algorithm SACA-K to compute the Lyndon array as a by-product of suffix array construction, referred to as SACA-K+LA.

We first recall the main steps of algorithm SACA-K (which is similar to *IS algorithm* shown in Fig. 6.1 and presented in Sect. 3.3.1).

Also, recall that whenever a suffix position is inserted at the tail (or head) of a c-bucket in SA, the pointer bkt[c] is increased (or decreased) by one.

Example Figure 6.2 shows a running example of algorithm SACA-K for the string $T = $ banaanananaanana$.

The key observation to adapt SACA-K to also compute the Lyndon array is that all LA values can be computed directly during Step 4 (at the top recursive level) when the suffixes are scanned in their final positions in SA.

Recall that the length of the longest Lyndon factor starting at position SA[i] in T is ℓ, and then LA[SA[i]] $= \ell$, if $T_{SA[i]+\ell}$ is the next suffix (in text order) that is smaller than $T_{SA[i]}$ (Remarks 2.1 and 2.2).

In Step 4, SA is scanned from right-to-left and the suffixes are read in decreasing order, that is, from SA[n], SA[$n - 1$], ..., SA[1], such that each value SA[i] is in

---

Steps:

1. Sort the LMS-suffixes and store in an auxiliary array SA^R.

2. Scan SA^R from right to left, $i = n^R, n^R - 1, \ldots, 1$, and insert each corresponding LMS-suffix of T into the tail of its c-bucket in SA.

3. Scan SA from left to right, $i = 1, 2, \ldots, n$, and for each suffix $T_{SA[i]}$, if $T_{SA[i]-1}$ is an L-suffix, insert SA[i] $- 1$ into the head of its bucket.

4. Scan SA from right to left , $i = n, n - 1, \ldots, 1$, and for each suffix $T_{SA[i]}$, if $T_{SA[i]-1}$ is an S-suffix, insert SA[i] $- 1$ into the tail of its bucket.

Fig. 6.1 *IS algorithm*

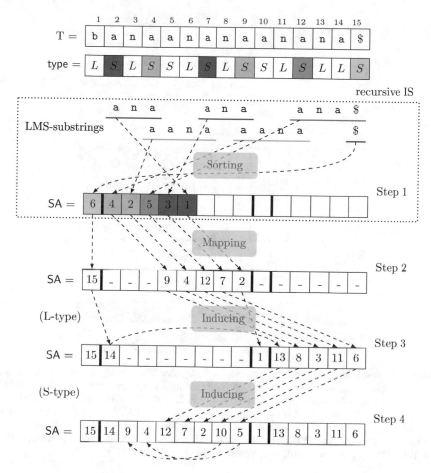

Fig. 6.2 Running example of algorithm SACA-K for $T =$ banaananaanana$ (refer to Sect. 3.3.1 for further examples)

its final (correct) position i in SA (see Sect. 3.3.1 for details). Therefore, whenever SA[i] is read, we can compute LA[SA[i]] by scanning positions LA[SA[i] + 1, n] to the right, up to the first position LA[SA[i] + ℓ] = 0, which means that SA[i] + ℓ has not been read yet (in Step 4), and as consequence $T_{SA[i]+\ell} < T_{SA[i]}$. Then, we set LA[SA[$i$]] = ℓ.

The correctness of this procedure follows from the fact that every position in LA[$1, n$] is initialized with zero, and if LA[SA[i] + 1], LA[SA[i] + 2], ..., LA[SA[i] + ℓ − 1] are not equal to zero, their corresponding suffixes have already been read in positions larger than i in SA[i + 1, n], and such suffixes are lexicographically larger than $T_{SA[i]}$. Then, the first position where we find LA[SA[i] + ℓ] = 0 corresponds to a suffix $T_{SA[i]+\ell}$ that is smaller than $T_{SA[i]}$. Also, $T_{SA[i]+\ell}$ is the next smaller suffix (in text order) because we read LA[SA[i] + 1, n] from left to right.

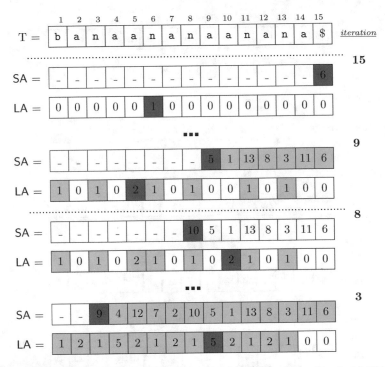

Fig. 6.3 Running example of the computation of the Lyndon array during Step 4 of SACA-K+LA for T = banaananaanana$. In this step SA is scanned from right to left and S-suffixes are induced (see Fig. 6.2). For example, at iteration $i = 9$, the suffix T_5 is read at position SA[9] and the corresponding value LA[5] is computed by scanning LA[6], LA[7], ..., LA[15] until finding the first empty position, which occurs at LA[5 + 2 = 7]. Therefore, LA[5] = 2. At iteration $i = 3$ we have a longer scan over LA, the suffix T_9 is read at position SA[3], and LA is scanned from LA[10], LA[11], ... up to LA[14] = 0. Thus LA[9] = 14 − 9 = 5

Example Figure 6.3 illustrates iterations $i = 15, 14, 9, 8, 4$ and 3 of modified Step 4 of algorithm SACA-K+LA, when SA is scanned from right to left and S-suffixes are induced.

Complexity Analysis
The running time of SACA-K+LA is $O(n \cdot \text{avelyn})$ time, where avelyn $= \sum_{i=1}^{n} \text{LA}[i]/n$, since at each iteration $i = n, n - 1, \ldots, 1$, the value of LA[SA[i]] is computed in additional LA[SA[i]] steps, that is $O(\text{LA}[i])$ extra time for each iteration of Step 4 of SACA-K. In the worst case, LA[i] = $n-i$, for $i = 1, \ldots, n-1$, LA[n] = 1 and the algorithm runs in $O(n^2)$ time.

The workspace of SACA-K+LA is $\sigma + O(1)$ words, the same as SACA-K, since no extra memory is needed in addition to the space for LA[1, n].

6.2.1 LA in Linear Time

In this section we show how to improve the running time of the algorithm presented in Sect. 6.2 such that each LA value is computed in constant time while increasing the workspace of the algorithm. We store two additional pointer arrays NEXT[1, n] and PREV[1, n], defined as follows.

Definition 6.1 NEXT[i] = min{$\ell | i < \ell \leq n$ and LA[ℓ] = 0}, for $i = 1, \ldots, n - 1$, and NEXT[n] = $n + 1$.

Definition 6.2 PREV[i] = ℓ provided that NEXT[ℓ] = i and LA[ℓ] = 0, for $i = 2, \ldots, n$, and PREV[1] = 0.

The arrays NEXT and PREV are updated at each iteration of Step 4, as SA is scanned and LA values are computed. Initially, NEXT[i] = $i + 1$ and PREV[i] = $i - 1$, for $1 \leq i \leq n$. Then, at each iteration $i = n, n - 1, \ldots, 1$, we scan SA[i] = j and compute LA[j] in constant time as

$$LA[j] = NEXT[j] - j \tag{6.1}$$

and the pointers arrays are updated as

$$NEXT[PREV[j]] = NEXT[j], \quad \text{if } PREV[j] > 0, \tag{6.2}$$

$$PREV[NEXT[j]] = PREV[j], \quad \text{if } NEXT[j] < n + 1. \tag{6.3}$$

In other words, at iteration i, SA[i] = j, and NEXT[j] gives the next smaller position ℓ in LA such that LA[ℓ] = 0, with $j < \ell$. Thus LA[j] = NEXT[j] − j is the length of the longest Lyndon factor starting at i. Symmetrically, PREV[j] gives the previous position in LA equal to zero which is used to update NEXT in constant time through the algorithm.

Example Figure 6.4 illustrates iterations $i = 15, 9, 8$ and 3 of Step 4 with the arrays PREV and NEXT.

Complexity Analysis
The running time of SACA-K+LA is now $O(n)$, the same as SACA-K. The cost to compute each LA value is constant, since only two additional computations (Eqs. 6.2 and 6.3) are needed, so that at iteration i, LA[SA[i]] is given by Eq. 6.1.

The workspace of SACA-K+LA increased to $2n + \sigma + O(1)$ words, since $2n$ extra words are needed to store arrays PREV and NEXT.

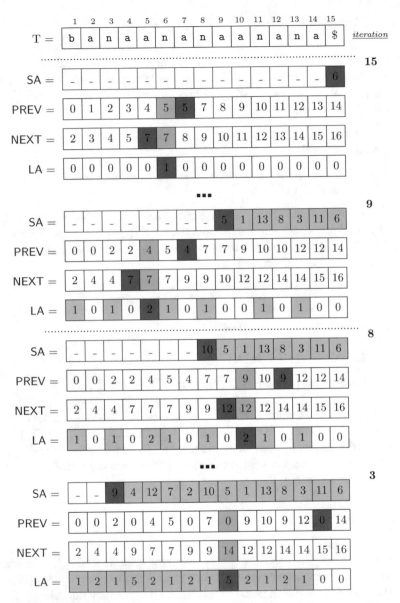

Fig. 6.4 Running example using arrays PREV and NEXT to compute the Lyndon array in linear time during Step 4 of SACA-K+LA for $T = $ banaananaanana$. At each iteration i positions in red are updated, and positions in green are used to compute LA[SA[i]] and update PREV and NEXT. For example, at iteration $i = 9$, the suffix T_5 is read at position SA[9], and LA[5] is computed as LA[5] = NEXT[5] $- 5 = 7 - 5 = 2$ (Eq. 6.1). The corresponding values in NEXT and PREV are updated accordingly, NEXT[4] = 7 and PREV[7] = 4 (Eqs. 6.2 and 6.3). At iteration $i = 3$, no value in NEXT is updated, since PREV[9] = 0

6.2.2 Eliminating a Pointer Array

Now, we show how to reduce the workspace of the algorithm of Sect. 6.2.1 by storing only one array, say $A[1, n]$, encoding NEXT and PREV information together.

The key idea is to initially store NEXT in the space of $A[1, n]$, then reusing $A[1, n]$ to store only useful entries of PREV.

Note that whenever we set $LA[j] = NEXT[j] - j$, the value in $A[j]$, namely $NEXT[j]$, is no longer used by the algorithm. See the green positions highlighted in Fig. 6.4. Then, we can reuse these $A[j]$ positions to store $PREV[j + 1]$. Also, we know that if $LA[j] = 0$, then $PREV[j + 1] = j$ (Definition 6.3). Therefore, we can redefine NEXT and PREV in terms of A and LA as

$$NEXT[j] = \begin{cases} A[j] & \text{if } LA[j] = 0 \\ \textit{undefined} & \text{otherwise} \end{cases} \qquad (6.4)$$

$$PREV[j] = \begin{cases} j - 1 & \text{if } LA[j - 1] = 0 \\ A[j - 1] & \text{otherwise.} \end{cases} \qquad (6.5)$$

The *undefined* values in NEXT are never used by the algorithm, since $LA[j]$ has been already computed. NEXT and PREV are updated in the space of $A[1, n]$, according to Eqs. 6.2 and 6.3 in constant time.

Example Figure 6.5 illustrates iterations $i = 15, 9, 8$ and 3 of Step 4 with array $A[1, n]$ encoding simultaneously PREV and NEXT.

Complexity Analysis
The running time of the algorithm remains the same, that is $O(n)$, since we have added only one extra verification to obtain $PREV[j]$ (Eq. 6.5) and undefined values in NEXT are never accessed by the algorithm.

The workspace is reduced to $n + \sigma + O(1)$ words, since only one integer array of size n is needed in addition to T, SA, and LA.

6.2.3 LA in Optimal Time and Space

In this section we show how to further reduce the workspace of the algorithm of Sect. 6.2.2 to $\sigma + O(1)$ words, that is, the same as SACA-K, which is optimal for strings from constant alphabets.

The key idea is that we can obtain the final values of LA by scanning $A[1, n]$ at the end of Step 4. Then $A[1, n]$ may be computed in the same space of LA.

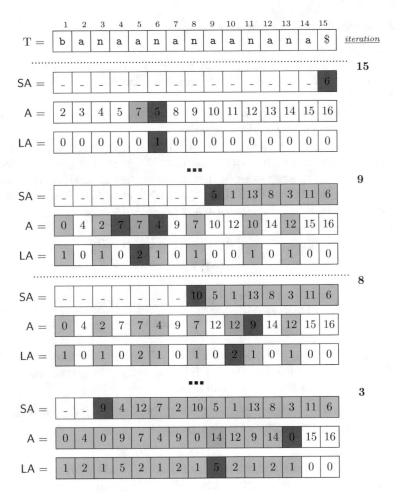

Fig. 6.5 Running example with array A[1, n] encoding **PREV** and **NEXT** to compute the Lyndon array in linear time during Step 4 of SACA-K+LA for $T = $ banaananaanana$. At each iteration i, positions in red are updated, and positions in green are no longer needed by the algorithm. For example, at iteration $i = 9$, the suffix T_5 is read at position SA[9], and LA[5] is computed as LA[5] = A[5] − 5 = 7 − 5 = 2 (Eqs. 6.1 and 6.4). The corresponding values in A that encodes **NEXT** and **PREV** are updated as NEXT[4] = A[4] = 7 and PREV[7] = A[6] = 4. At iteration $i = 15$, LA[6] = A[6] − 6 = 7 − 6 = 1 and A[6] is overwritten to store PREV[7] = 5

First, observe that if T_i is an L-suffix, then LA[j] = 1, since $T_j > T_{j+1}$ (Definition 3.3 and Remark 2.1). Then, it is easy to compute LA values of L-suffixes at the end of Step 4.

In Step 4, during iteration $i = n, n − 1, \ldots, 1$, whenever we read an S-suffix T_j, with $j = $ SA[i], its succeeding suffix (in text order) T_{j+1} has already been read at some position in the interval SA[$i + 1, n$], since $T_j < T_{j+1}$ and T_{j+1} have induced the order of T_j. Therefore, the LA entries corresponding to S-suffixes are always inserted on the left of a block (possibly of size one) of non-zero entries in LA[1, n].

See LA-positions highlighted in red in Fig. 6.5 during iterations 9, 8, and 3, as an example.

Moreover, whenever we compute $LA[j] = \ell$, we have $NEXT[j] = j+\ell$ stored in $A[j]$, which means that entries $LA[j+1], LA[j+2], \ldots, LA[j+\ell-1]$ are no longer zero, and we only have to update $A[j+\ell-1]$, corresponding to the information of $PREV[j+\ell]$ (Eq. 6.7). In other words, we update $A[1, n]$ with PREV information only for rightmost entry of each block of non-empty entries, which correspond to positions of L-suffixes because S-suffixes are always inserted at the left of a block.

We may also redefine NEXT and PREV in terms of A only as

$$NEXT[j] = \begin{cases} A[j] & \text{if } A[j] > j \\ undefined & \text{otherwise} \end{cases} \qquad (6.6)$$

$$PREV[j] = \begin{cases} j - 1 & \text{if } A[j - 1] > j \\ A[j - 1] & \text{otherwise.} \end{cases} \qquad (6.7)$$

At the end of Step 4, if $A[j] < j$, then T_j is an L-suffix, and we know that $LA[j] = 1$. On the other hand, the values with $A[j] > j$ remain equal to $NEXT[j]$ at the end of the algorithm, since we only overwrite values in $A[1, n]$ with PREV information when T_j is an L-suffix. Therefore, after the completion of Step 4, we sequentially scan $A[1, n]$ overwriting its values with LA as

$$LA[j] = \begin{cases} 1 & \text{if } A[j] < j \\ A[j] - j & \text{otherwise.} \end{cases} \qquad (6.8)$$

Example Figure 6.6 illustrates iterations $i = 15, 9, 8, 3$ and 1 of Step 4 with array $A[1, n]$ being overwritten with values of LA at the end.

Complexity Analysis

The running time of the algorithm remains $O(n)$, since only an additional linear scan over $A[1, n]$ at the end of Step 4 is performed.

On the other hand, the workspace is reduced to $O\sigma + O(1)$ words since the extra space used for $A[1, n]$ is no longer needed, as $A[1, n]$ is overwritten by LA.

We remark that the bounds on the workspace given in this section assume that the output consists of SA and LA. If one is interested in LA only, then the workspace of the algorithm is $n + \sigma + O(1)$ words which is still smaller that the workspace of the other linear time algorithms available in the literature.

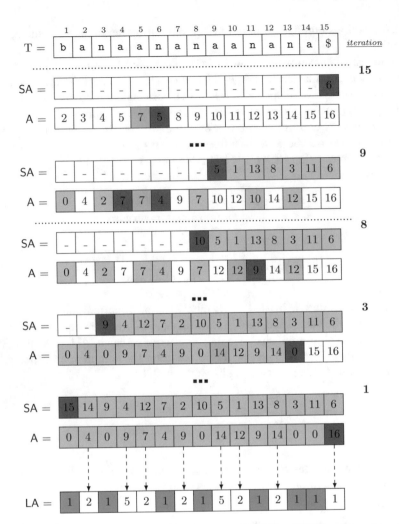

Fig. 6.6 Running example with array $A[1, n]$ encoding **PREV** and **NEXT** and reused to compute **LA** after the end of Step 4 of SACA-K+LA for $T =$ banaananaanana$. The final **LA** is presented at the bottom. At the end of iteration 1, $A[1, n]$ is scanned sequentially and its values are overwritten by the Lyndon array. Positions in blue correspond to the L-suffixes, which **LA** values are always 1. The other **LA** entries correspond to the S-suffixes, and their values are computed by Eq. 6.8. For example, $LA[9] = A[9] - 9 = 14 - 9 = 5$

6.3 Experiments

In this section we compare the performance of SACA-K+LA [16] with other linear time algorithms that compute only **LA**. We evaluated algorithms by Franek et al. [11], Baier [1, 9], and Louza et al. [17]. We also compared a version of Baier's algorithm that computes both **LA** and **SA**.

Table 6.1 Running time (μs/input byte). Column 2 shows the alphabet size. Column 3 shows the collection size in MB

| Dataset | σ | $n/2^{20}$ | LA | | | LA and SA | | | | SA |
			NSV-LYNDON [11]	BAIER-LA [1,9]	BWT-LYNDON [17]	BAIER-LA+SA [1,9]	SACA-K+LA-17n	SACA-K+LA-13n	SACA-K+LA-9n	SACA-K [21]
sources	230	201	**0.26**	0.28	0.32	0.37	0.46	0.41	**0.34**	0.24
xml	97	282	**0.29**	0.31	0.35	0.42	0.52	0.47	**0.38**	0.27
dna	16	385	0.39	**0.28**	0.49	**0.43**	0.69	0.60	0.52	0.36
english.1GB	239	1,047	0.46	**0.39**	0.56	**0.57**	0.84	0.74	0.60	0.42
proteins	27	1,129	0.44	**0.40**	0.53	0.66	0.89	0.69	**0.58**	0.40
einstein-de	117	88	0.34	**0.28**	0.38	**0.39**	0.57	0.54	0.44	0.31
kernel	160	246	0.29	**0.29**	0.39	**0.38**	0.53	0.47	**0.38**	0.26
fib41	2	256	0.34	**0.07**	0.45	**0.18**	0.66	0.57	0.46	0.32
cere	5	440	0.27	**0.09**	0.33	**0.17**	0.43	0.41	0.35	0.25
bbba	2	100	0.04	**0.02**	0.05	**0.03**	0.05	0.04	**0.03**	0.03

The best results are shown in bold

We considered the three linear time alternatives of SACA-K+LA, described in Sects. 6.2.1, 6.2.2, and 6.2.3, denoted according to their total peakspace, respectively, $17n$, $13n$, and $9n$ bytes. We also included the performance of algorithm SACA-K [21] that computes only SA to assess the overhead added by the computation of LA in SACA-K+LA.

SACA-K+LA was implemented in ANSI C based on the source codes of SACA-K.[1] The source codes are publicly available at https://github.com/felipelouza/lyndon-array/.

We used string collections from the Pizza & Chili dataset.[2] In particular, datasets einstein-de, kernel, fib41, and cere are highlyrepetitive,[3] and the english.1G is the first 1GB of the original english dataset. We also created an artificial repetitive dataset, called bbba, consisting of a string T with 100×2^{20} copies of symbol b followed by one occurrence of symbol a, that is, $T = b^{n-2}a\$$. This dataset represents a worst-case input for the algorithms that use an auxiliary stack (e.g. [11, 17]).

The experiments were conducted on a machine with Debian GNU/Linux 8 (kernel 3.16.0-4) 64 bits operating system with an Intel Xeon processor

---

[1] code.google.com/archive/p/ge-nong/downloads.

[2] http://pizzachili.dcc.uchile.cl/texts.html.

[3] http://pizzachili.dcc.uchile.cl/repcorpus.html.

Table 6.2 Peakspace (bytes/input size). Column 2 shows the alphabet size. Column 3 shows the collection size in MB

Dataset	σ	$n/2^{20}$	LA			LA and SA				SA
			NSV-LYNDON [11]	BAIER-LA [1, 9]	BWT-LYNDON [17]	BAIER-LA+SA [1, 9]	SACA-K+LA-17n	SACA-K+LA-13n	SACA-K+LA-9n	SACA-K [21]
sources	230	201	**9**	17	**9**	17	17	13	**9**	5
xml	97	282	**9**	17	**9**	17	17	13	**9**	5
dna	16	385	**9**	17	**9**	17	17	13	**9**	5
english.1GB	239	1,047	**9**	17	**9**	17	17	13	**9**	5
proteins	27	1,129	**9**	17	**9**	17	17	13	**9**	5
einstein-de	117	88	**9**	17	**9**	17	17	13	**9**	5
kernel	160	246	**9**	17	**9**	17	17	13	**9**	5
fib41	2	256	**9**	17	**9**	17	17	13	**9**	5
cere	5	440	**9**	17	**9**	17	17	13	**9**	5
bbba	2	100	**13**	17	17	17	17	13	**9**	5

The best results are shown in bold

E5-2630 v3 2.40-GHz with 20 MB of cache, 386 GB of RAM, and a 13 TB SATA storage. The time was measured with clock() function of C standard libraries and the memory was measured using malloc_count library.[4]

Running Time

Table 6.1 shows the running time of each algorithm in μs/symbol. The performance of SACA-K+LA-9n and BAIER-LA+SA [1, 9] was very similar. In particular, SACA-K+LA-9n was only about 1.35 times slower than the fastest algorithm (BAIER-LA) for non-repetitive datasets, and 2.92 times slower for repetitive datasets.

Note that SACA-K+LA-9n was consistently faster than SACA-K+LA-13n and SACA-K+LA-17n, so using more space does not yield any advantage. Finally, the overhead of computing LA in addition to SA was small: SACA-K+LA-9n was 1.42 times slower than SACA-K, whereas BAIER-LA+SA was 1.55 times slower than BAIER-LA, on average.

Peakspace

Table 6.2 shows the peak memory usage of each algorithm in bytes per input symbol. NSV-LYNDON [11], BWT-LYNDON [17], and SACA-K+LA-9n presented the smallest values. The space used by NSV-LYNDON and BWT-LYNDON was $9n$

---

[4]https://github.com/bingmann/malloc_count.

Table 6.3 Workspace in MB, except for SACA-K+LA-9n and SACA-K, which used exactly 1 KB. Column 2 shows the alphabet size. Column 3 shows the collection size in MB

| Dataset | σ | $n/2^{70}$ | LA | | | LA and SA | | | | SA |
			NSV-LYNDON [11]	BAIER-LA [1, 9]	BWT-LYNDON [17]	BAIER-LA+SA [1, 9]	SACA-K+LA-17n	SACA-K+LA-13n	SACA-K+LA-9n	SACA-K [21]
sources	230	201	**804.4**	2, 413.2	**804.4**	1, 608.8	1, 608.8	804.4	**1**	1
xml	97	282	**1,129.7**	3, 389.0	**1,129.7**	2, 259.3	2, 259.3	1, 129.7	**1**	1
dna	16	385	**1,540.9**	4, 622.6	**1,540.9**	3, 081.7	3, 081.7	1, 540.9	**1**	1
english.1GB	239	1,047	**4,187.4**	2, 562.2	**4,187.4**	8, 374.8	8, 374.8	4, 187.4	**1**	1
proteins	27	1,129	**4,516.8**	3, 550.4	**4,516.8**	9, 033.6	9, 033.6	4, 516.8	**1**	1
einstein-de	117	88	**353.9**	1, 061.5	**353.9**	707.7	707.7	353.8	**1**	1
kernel	160	246	**984.1**	2, 952.1	**984.1**	1, 968.1	1, 968.1	984.0	**1**	1
fib41	2	256	**1,022.0**	3, 066.0	**1,022.0**	2, 044.0	2, 044.0	1, 022.0	**1**	1
cere	5	440	**1,759.9**	5, 279.0	**1,759.9**	3, 519.3	3, 519.3	1, 759.7	**1**	1
bbba	2	100	1,200.0	1, 200.0	1,200.0	800.0	800.0	400.0	**1**	1

The best results are shown in bold

bytes plus the space used by a stack of integers. The stack space was negligible (about 10KB) for almost all datasets, except for bbba where the stack used $4n$ bytes for NSV-LYNDON and $8n$ bytes for BWT-LYNDON (the number of stack entries is the same, but BWT-LYNDON's stack entries consist of a pair of integers).

On the other hand, SACA-K+LA-9n used exactly $9n + 1024$ bytes for all datasets.

Workspace

Table 6.3 shows the workspace of each algorithm in MB, except for algorithms SACA-K+LA-9n and SACA-K, whose workspace was exactly equal to 1 KB. The workspace was obtained by subtracting from peakspace the space used by T and the output. We considered three different scenarios. First, only LA is output, then LA and SA, and finally only SA.

The smallest values were given by SACA-K+LA-9n, which was the only solution that kept the workspace constant. The additional space used by NSV-LYNDON and BWT-LYNDON was equal to that used by SACA-K+LA-13n, except on bbba. For dataset bbba we can see that solutions that compute LA and SA use less additional space than solutions that obtain only LA.

Conclusions

Overall, SACA-K+LA, especially the lightweight version SACA-K+LA-9n, provides a good space efficient alternative compared to the other linear time solutions to compute the Lyndon array, which shows that SACA-K+LA is competitive in practice.

References

1. U. Baier, Linear-time suffix sorting - a new approach for suffix array construction, in *Proc. Annual Symposium on Combinatorial Pattern Matching (CPM)*, pp. 23:1–23:12 (2016)
2. H. Bannai, I. Tomohiro, S. Inenaga, Y. Nakashima, M. Takeda, K. Tsuruta, The "runs" theorem. SIAM J. Comput. **46**(5), 1501–1514 (2017)
3. T. Beller, M. Zwerger, S. Gog, E. Ohlebusch, Space-efficient construction of the Burrows–Wheeler transform, in *Proc. International Symposium on String Processing and Information Retrieval (SPIRE)*, pp. 5–16 (Springer International Publishing, 2013)
4. M. Crochemore, L.M.S. Russo, Cartesian and Lyndon trees. Theor. Comput. Sci. (2018)
5. J. Fischer, Inducing the LCP-array, in *Proc. Workshop on Algorithms and Data Structures (WADS)*, pp. 374–385 (2011)
6. F. Franek, A.S.M. Sohidull Islam, M.S. Rahman, W.F. Smyth, Algorithms to compute the Lyndon array, in *Proc. Prague Stringology Conference (PSC)*, pp. 172–184 (2016)
7. F. Franek, M. Liut, Algorithms to compute the Lyndon array revisited, in *Proc. Prague Stringology Conference (PSC)*, pp. 16–28 (2019)
8. F. Franek, M. Liut, W.F. Smyth, On Baier's sort of maximal Lyndon substrings, in *Proc. Prague Stringology Conference (PSC)*, pp. 63–78 (2018)
9. F. Franek, A. Paracha, W.F. Smyth, The linear equivalence of the suffix array and the partially sorted Lyndon array, in *Proc. Prague Stringology Conference (PSC)*, pp. 77–84 (2017)
10. K. Goto, H. Bannai, Space efficient linear time Lempel-Ziv factorization for small alphabets, in *Proc. IEEE Data Compression Conference (DCC)*, pp. 163–172 (2014)
11. C. Hohlweg, C. Reutenauer, Lyndon words, permutations and trees. Theor. Comput. Sci. **307**(1), 173–178 (2003)
12. J. Kärkkäinen, Suffix array construction, in *Encyclopedia of Algorithms*, pp. 2141–2144 (Springer, 2016)
13. R.M. Kolpakov, G. Kucherov, Finding maximal repetitions in a word in linear time, in *Proc. Annual IEEE Symposium on Foundations of Computer Science (FOCS)*, pp. 596–604 (1999)
14. F.A. Louza, S. Gog, G.P. Telles, Inducing enhanced suffix arrays for string collections. Theor. Comput. Sci. **678**, 22–39 (2017)
15. F.A. Louza, S. Gog, G.P. Telles, Optimal suffix sorting and LCP array construction for constant alphabets. Inf. Process. Lett. **118**, 30–34 (2017)
16. F.A. Louza, S. Mantaci, G. Manzini, M. Sciortino, G.P. Telles, Inducing the Lyndon array, in *Proc. International Symposium on String Processing and Information Retrieval (SPIRE)*, pp. 138–151 (2019)
17. F.A. Louza, W.F. Smyth, G. Manzini, G.P. Telles, Lyndon array construction during Burrows-Wheeler inversion. J. Discrete Algorithms **50**, 2–9 (2018)
18. V. Mäkinen, D. Belazzougui, F. Cunial, A.I. Tomescu, *Genome-Scale Algorithm Design* (Cambridge University Press, 2015)
19. U. Manber, G. Myers, Suffix arrays: a new method for on-line string searches, in *Proc. ACM-SIAM Symposium on Discrete Algorithms (SODA)*, pp. 319–327 (1990)
20. G. Navarro, *Compact Data Structures: A Practical Approach* (Cambridge University Press, 2016)
21. G. Nong, Practical linear-time O(1)-workspace suffix sorting for constant alphabets. ACM Trans. Inf. Syst. **31**(3), 1–15 (2013)

22. G. Nong, S. Zhang, W.H. Chan, Two efficient algorithms for linear time suffix array construction. IEEE Trans. Comput. **60**(10), 1471–1484 (2011)
23. D.S.N. Nunes, F.A. Louza, S. Gog, M. Ayala-Rincón, G. Navarro, A grammar compression algorithm based on induced suffix sorting, in *Proc. IEEE Data Compression Conference (DCC)*, pp. 42–51 (2018)
24. E. Ohlebusch, *Bioinformatics Algorithms: Sequence Analysis, Genome Rearrangements and Phylogenetic Reconstruction* (Oldenbusch Verlag, 2013)
25. D. Okanohara, K. Sadakane, A linear-time Burrows-Wheeler transform using induced sorting, in *Proc. International Symposium on String Processing and Information Retrieval (SPIRE)*, vol. 5721 of *LNCS*, pp. 90–101 (Springer, 2009)
26. S.J. Puglisi, W.F. Smyth, A.H. Turpin, A taxonomy of suffix array construction algorithms. ACM Comput. Surv. **39**(2), 1–31 (2007)

Part III
Conclusions

Chapter 7
Conclusions

7.1 Contributions and Future Works

In this book we presented recent theoretical and practical advances for three different problems of wide interest in string processing. Specifically, we presented augmented suffix sorting algorithms to compute the suffix array together with the longest common prefix (LCP) array (Chap. 4), the document array (Chap. 5), and the Lyndon array (Chap. 6). All presented solutions are optimal in time and space for strings from alphabets of constant size $\sigma = O(1)$.

In Chap. 4 we presented an algorithm that computes the LCP array together with the suffix array in $O(n\sigma)$ time using $4\sigma + O(1)$ words of workspace. The algorithm, called SACA-K+LCP [14], can be viewed as a refinement of Fischer's ideas [4] (also described in Chap. 4) to compute the LCP array during algorithm SACA-K [16], with a more careful usage of the available memory. Overall, this result presents an improvement for the simultaneous construction of suffix and LCP arrays. As future work one can investigate whether other suffix array construction algorithms (e.g. [1, 5, 11]) can be adapted to compute the LCP array during suffix sorting.

In Chap. 5 we presented algorithms for string collections. We showed how to modify the algorithms SAIS [19] and SACA-K [16] to construct generalized suffix arrays maintaining their theoretical bounds. As a result, the algorithm, called gSACA-K [13], runs in $O(N)$ time using only $\sigma + O(1)$ words of workspace for a collection of total length N, which is optimal for strings from constant alphabets. We also showed how to compute the document array during suffix sorting, with no asymptotic slowdown. The algorithm, called gSACA-K+DA, improves the theoretical complexity of the solution and represents practical advances in building indexes for string collections. As future work one can investigate whether algorithms that compute data structures for single strings can be modified to handle string collections (e.g. [3, 6, 7, 12, 15, 17, 20–22]).

F. A. Louza et al., *Construction of Fundamental Data Structures for Strings*,
SpringerBriefs in Computer Science, https://doi.org/10.1007/978-3-030-55108-7_7

In Chap. 6 we presented an algorithm that computes the Lyndon array during suffix sorting in $O(n)$ time using $n + \sigma + O(1)$ words of workspace. The algorithm, called SACA-K+LA, is a modification of SACA-K [16] to compute the Lyndon array. If one is interested in both suffix and Lyndon arrays, then the workspace of SACA-K+LA is $\sigma + O(1)$ words, which is optimal for constant alphabets. SACA-K+LA is one of the most space economical Lyndon array construction alternatives among the ones running in linear time, including both the algorithm computing the suffix and Lyndon arrays and the ones computing only the Lyndon array. Very recently, Bille et al. [2] showed how to compute the Lyndon array directly (without suffix arrays) in linear time using only $O(1)$ words of working space. As future work one can compare the practical performance of Bille et al.'s algorithm with SACA-K+LA.

There exist different alternatives that adapt algorithms SAIS and SACA-K to other computer models, like external memory (e.g. [3, 7, 12, 17, 18, 23]) and parallel computing (e.g.[8–10, 24]). As future work one can investigate if these variants can be adapted to also compute the data structures investigated in this book during suffix sorting.

References

1. U. Baier, Linear-time suffix sorting - a new approach for suffix array construction, in *Proc. Annual Symposium on Combinatorial Pattern Matching (CPM)*, pp. 23:1–23:12 (2016)
2. P. Bille, J. Ellert, J. Fischer, I.L. Gørtz, F. Kurpicz, J. Ian Munro, E. Rotenberg, Space efficient construction of Lyndon arrays in linear time. CoRR (2019). abs/1911.03542
3. T. Bingmann, J. Fischer, V. Osipov, Inducing suffix and LCP arrays in external memory. J. Exp. Algorithmics **21**(2), 2.3:1–2.3:27 (2016)
4. J. Fischer, Inducing the LCP-array, in *Proc. Workshop on Algorithms and Data Structures (WADS)*, pp. 374–385 (2011)
5. K. Goto, Optimal time and space construction of suffix arrays and LCP arrays for integer alphabets, in *Proc. Prague Stringology Conference (PSC)*, pp. 111–125 (2019)
6. K. Goto, H. Bannai, Space efficient linear time Lempel-Ziv factorization for small alphabets, in *Proc. IEEE Data Compression Conference (DCC)*, pp. 163–172 (2014)
7. J. Kärkkäinen, D. Kempa, S.J. Puglisi, B. Zhukova, Engineering external memory induced suffix sorting, in *Proc. Workshop on Algorithm Engineering and Experimentation (ALENEX)*, pp. 98–108 (2017)
8. J. Labeit, J. Shun, G.E. Blelloch, Parallel lightweight wavelet tree, suffix array and FM-index construction. J. Discrete Algorithms **43**, 2–17 (2017)
9. B. Lao, G. Nong, W.H. Chan, Y. Pan, Fast induced sorting suffixes on a multicore machine. J. Supercomput. **74**(7), 3468–3485 (2018)
10. B. Lao, G. Nong, W.H. Chan, J.Y. Xie, Fast in-place suffix sorting on a multicore computer. IEEE Trans. Comput. **67**(12), 1737–1749 (2018)
11. Z. Li, J. Li, H. Huo, Optimal in-place suffix sorting, in *Proc. International Symposium on String Processing and Information Retrieval (SPIRE)*, pp. 268–284 (2018)
12. W.J. Liu, G. Nong, W.H. Chan, Y. Wu, Induced sorting suffixes in external memory with better design and less space, in *Proc. International Symposium on String Processing and Information Retrieval (SPIRE)*, pp. 83–94 (2015)

13. F.A. Louza, S. Gog, G.P. Telles, Inducing enhanced suffix arrays for string collections. Theor. Comput. Sci. **678**, 22–39 (2017)
14. F.A. Louza, S. Gog, G.P. Telles, Optimal suffix sorting and LCP array construction for constant alphabets. Inf. Process. Lett. **118**, 30–34 (2017)
15. F.A. Louza, S. Mantaci, G. Manzini, M. Sciortino, G.P. Telles, Inducing the Lyndon array, in *Proc. International Symposium on String Processing and Information Retrieval (SPIRE)*, pp. 138–151 (2019)
16. G. Nong, Practical linear-time O(1)-workspace suffix sorting for constant alphabets. ACM Trans. Inf. Syst. **31**(3), 1–15 (2013)
17. G. Nong, W.H. Chan, S.Q. Hu, Y. Wu, Induced sorting suffixes in external memory. ACM Trans. Inf. Syst. **33**(3), 12:1–12:15 (2015)
18. G. Nong, W.H. Chan, S. Zhang, X.F. Guan, Suffix array construction in external memory using d-critical substrings. ACM Trans. Inf. Syst. **32**, 1:1–1:15 (2014)
19. G. Nong, S. Zhang, W.H. Chan, Two efficient algorithms for linear time suffix array construction. IEEE Trans. Comput. **60**(10), 1471–1484 (2011)
20. D. Okanohara, K. Sadakane, A linear-time Burrows-Wheeler transform using induced sorting, in *Proc. International Symposium on String Processing and Information Retrieval (SPIRE)*, vol. 5721 of *LNCS*, pp. 90–101 (Springer, 2009)
21. N. Prezza, G. Rosone, Space-efficient computation of the LCP array from the Burrows-Wheeler transform. CoRR (2019). abs/1901.05226
22. J.F. Sepúlveda, G. Navarro, Y. Nekrich, Space-efficient computation of the Burrows-Wheeler transform, in *Proc. IEEE Data Compression Conference (DCC)*, pp. 132–141 (2019)
23. Y. Wu, B. Lao, X. Ma, G. Nong, An improved algorithm for building suffix array in external memory, in *Proc. International Symposium on Parallel Architectures, Algorithms and Programming (PAAP)*, pp. 320–330 (2019)
24. J.Y. Xie, B. Lao, G. Nong, In-place suffix sorting on a multicore computer with better design, in *Proc. International Symposium on Parallel Architectures, Algorithms and Programming (PAAP)*, pp. 331–342 (2019)

Index

Printed in the United States
By Bookmasters